RSPB
CHILDREN'S GUIDE TO
Nature
Watching

A & C BLACK
AN IMPRINT OF BLOOMSBURY
LONDON NEW DELHI NEW YORK SYDNEY

Published 2013 by
A&C Black
An imprint of Bloomsbury Publishing Plc
50 Bedford Square, London, WC1B 3DP

www.bloomsbury.com

ISBN 978-1-4081-8757-9

This book is produced using paper that is made from wood grown in managed, sustainable forests. It is natural, renewable and recyclable. The logging and manufacturing processes conform to the environmental regulations of the country of origin.

Printed in China by C&C Offset Printer Co.

10 9 8 7 6 5 4 3 2 1

MIX
Paper from
responsible sources
FSC® C008047
FSC
www.fsc.org

Contents

Introduction

Watching nature is fun. It can be exciting, it can be funny, and it is certainly fascinating. You can do it at home, at school, in your garden, from a car, train or bus. You can do it at any time of the year, and anywhere in the world. You can be a bit interested one day, and keen the next. You can spend hours and hours looking for wildlife, or just enjoy glimpses as you pass by doing something else.

Watching nature can also be useful. We need to know what's around us to know if any of it is in trouble and needs human help. And we also need to check that what we are doing to the natural world won't affect people too. But for now, just remember that nature watching is great fun and can inspire you for the rest of your life.

This is a book of three parts. The first part will help you to get the most out of nature. How to enjoy it. How to study it, what it is and what's worth looking for and when. It's all about helping you to become interested in wildlife.

The second part gives you a flavour of what to see in different habitats – woodlands, the seashore, and many more places.

The third part of the book tells you a bit about the wildlife that you are likely to see, or that is worth seeking out for some special reason. It has some of the most famous wildlife, but also some that you may never have come across. There is so much to discover!

There is plenty in here, but there's also lots more than this to look for! I hope you like my selection and that it makes you keen to discover more.

Mark Boyd

What is wildlife?

We all know that, don't we? Wildlife is any living creature, except human beings, that lives in the wild. So, a lion in the zoo isn't wild (even when it's rather cross), but a lion on the plains of Africa is wild, even when it's asleep. Pets and farm animals like dogs, hamsters, goldfish or sheep aren't wild. Their ancestors were wild, and they may do things in their own wild way, but we wouldn't call them wildlife.

What about the spider in your shed, or the weed in your flowerbed? These are still wild – they live their lives in places that suit them, but those just happen to be with us. They are as wild as your pet cat's fleas!

It's not always so easy. If gardeners grow a plant from abroad and it now grows where it likes, inside the garden and out, then it, too, has gone wild. And if people have brought plants or animals from abroad and let them go, either on purpose or by mistake, they will still seem wild. We call these non-natives, introductions or aliens – but they didn't come from outer space!

Sometimes what these non-natives do isn't welcome, from rabbits that eat a farmer's crops to rats and squirrels spreading diseases, but many are just colourful or interesting additions to our countryside, like golden pheasants and even apple trees. But wherever they first came from, they will all have their own fascinating stories for you to discover.

Nature is everywhere. In the countryside but also at home.

5

Being an active naturalist

You can enjoy the wildlife that you see day to day, or you can be an active naturalist. This means taking a special interest in the natural world, going places and doing things to increase your chances of seeing wildlife. And here's the thing. Active naturalists have more fun!

There are so many things to look for that many active naturalists do no more than learn the names of what they find. That's ok, but you don't have to stop there. Why not find out what wildlife you see does, what it eats and what eats it?

We know more about wildlife in the UK than anywhere else in the world, but every year new species are discovered. These might be windblown stray birds and insects that will never come back here again. However, some might be the start of a new wave of creatures that have moved in as our climate gets warmer or have been transported here with goods from other countries.

Every time you step outdoors, you can certainly find things that you have never seen before – you just have to choose to look.

Keep a record of your finds.

Starting out

Identifying wildlife sounds easy enough. It's just putting names to whatever you find. The trick is putting the same name to it that everyone else does! Identification is the starting point for all active naturalists. Once you know what something is called, you can find out more about it. You can then look it up in books or online and learn how what you find fits in with what else is known about the species.

For example, if you find an angle-shades moth on your wall in late November, you can look it up to see if that is a normal time of year to see the species. But first you have to know it's an angle-shades moth.

Is it a bird ... is it a plane tree?

The thing to remember when identifying wildlife is not to jump to conclusions and to use your common sense. Keep your options open. Only start to narrow your search down when you are sure you have picked the right group – you probably wouldn't confuse a bird and a tree, but is that minibeast you have found an insect, a kind of spider or a woodlouse? Get this right first or you'll start inventing all sorts of strange things.

It's best to decide on the group by looking at the creature or plant itself. Don't, for example, think that just because you saw a squirrel in the water, it's a watery creature – it may have fallen in!

Using a key

You can use a key to help, such as the one on the following two pages. A key is a process of questions and answers. So long as you get all the answers right, you can start to put a name to your creature. But be careful. One wrong answer and everything that follows it will also be wrong. So don't follow the key without thinking. After each answer ask yourself – does this still feel right?

Making your identification

Once you have decided which group your mystery wildlife falls into, you need to take it further – from animal to minibeast, to insect, to moth, to large moth, to angle-shades moth. The closer to making your identification you get, the more technical the language can become. Don't worry about that. It's only labelling that is there to help.

Keeping a record

Once you have taken your identification as far as you can on your own, it makes sense to record as much about it as you can. You can photograph it, write about it or draw what you have found. Drawing is often best because you can only draw something you have looked at properly.

Do this before looking it up, unless you can flick through a book with your mystery object still in view. Otherwise, when you start looking at the options you will start to doubt your own memory: how many legs did it really have? And what colour were they? If you have a record, you can look it up.

Checking your find

Now have a look in a suitable book that covers the wildlife in the area where you are looking (and preferably no wider). Were you correct about what you found?

A wildlife key

Answer each question truthfully and you can narrow down what you have found.
If you need more detail, invent more questions!

1 Is it a plant?

Probably green, not moving, maybe with flowers, twigs, seeds or nuts.

Yes   Go to 2.

No   Go to 7.

2 Is it a tree?

With a woody trunk or stem, branches, leaves, flowers or seeds, or surrounded by fallen leaves in winter. Woody bushes count as trees.

Yes   Go to 3.

No   Go to 4.

3 Is it a conifer tree?

With thin, needle-like leaves, probably all year around, but perhaps bare in winter with brown needles underneath on the ground.

Yes   Look up conifer trees on page 137.

No   Look up broad-leaved trees on page 138.

4 Is it a fern, moss, liverwort or seaweed?

Never with flowers, often in shaded, damp places, or washed up on the beach. Probably green, red or brown.

Yes   Look up 'lower' plants on pages 148-149.

No   Go to 5.

5 Does it look like a mushroom, with a cap and stem, or possibly growing out of the side of a tree or rotting wood?

Yes   Look up fungi on pages 150-152.

No   Probably a flowering plant. Go to 6.

6 Does it have, or look like it should have flowers? Be careful, they may be green, or tiny, or you may have found the plant outside its flowering season.

Yes   Look up flowering plants from pages 139-147.

No   Try 1-6 again, or perhaps 15, if it was really an animal.

7 Welcome to the world of animals. Let's start with the bigger ones. Did your creature have feathers?

Yes   It's a bird! Fly to pages 81-91.

No   Go to 8.

8 Does it have four feet and fur?

Yes   It's a mammal. Run along to pages 66-76.
No   Go to 9.

9 Does it have no arms or legs, have fins and looks happiest underwater?

Yes   Go to 10.
No   Go to 11.

10 Does it have scaly skin and gills at the sides of its head?

Yes   It's a fish. Swim along to pages 96-99.
No   It's a whale, dolphin or seal – all mammals without feet! See pages 77-79.

11 Does it have scaly skin and live on land, or at least look as though it could walk with its legs (if it had any)? If you saw it swimming, did it keep its nose out of the water?

Yes   Sounds like a reptile. Go to 12.
No   Sounds like an amphibian. Go to 13.

12 Does it have four legs?

Yes   See the lizards on page 92-94.
No   Slither along to the snakes and slow-worm, page 92-94.

13 Does it have a tail?

Yes   Check out the newts on page 95.
No   Hop along to page 95 for the frogs and toads.

Not one of the above? You will be looking at an invertebrate – an animal without a backbone. Go to 14.

14 Does it have legs?

Yes   Go to 15.
No   Go to 16.

15 Does it have six or eight legs?

Yes   You have an insect or spider. Scamper along to pages 100-123.
No   If it has lots more legs than that, check out the centipedes and millipedes on page 130, and the crustaceans on page 124-126.

16 Does it have an obvious shell?

Yes   Look up snails and shellfish on pages 127-129.
No   Sounds sluggy or wormy. See page 133-134.

If you want to go further than this, make up some more questions. Just remember they have to be answered 'yes' or 'no' with no confusing 'maybes'.

Beyond counting

Observing wildlife doesn't have to be about numbers. Counting is important, but it's not the only fun you can have as an active naturalist.

You could choose to photograph, draw or paint what you see, or write down observations, stories or poems based on it. This is more personal because you are responding to wildlife, not just recording it.

Observation ideas

- Draw a tree from memory. Now go and look at a real tree and draw it from what you are really seeing. Try to move your pencil across the page at the same speed as your eye moves along each branch. You will probably have a better picture as a result. Even if you haven't you will have looked at that tree very actively.

- Find somewhere where there are lots of animals of the same type – a bird table, duck pond, deer park – and try drawing each one. When it moves, switch to another creature, but still draw from life. You will soon notice that each creature is different.

- If you haven't got a fancy camera, don't worry. Most phones have cameras that are good enough to take pictures of flowers, fungi and slow-moving insects.

- Bring all this together in a nature diary or blog. Fill it with counts of what you see, but also write what you felt about the encounter. In a year's time that description will bring the memory flooding back. Remember to include a note of the date, the weather and the location for every record.

Drawing tips

One way to draw is to look hard at what you see and try to simplify it into shapes such as circles, squares and triangles. Get those down in the right sizes and then adjust each shape to fit what you are looking at.

Another way is to imagine that there is a window pane between you and your wildlife. Now, draw what's on the window pane – this can help to make the 3D world flatter and easier to draw.

All you really need to be a naturalist is a curious nature that gets you outside to see what we share our fantastic planet with. But you will get more out of it with a few key pieces of kit. You don't need all of this to get started, but try not to leave home without your essentials. It's best to keep some of these in your coat pockets rather than your backpack for easy access – and if you have binoculars, they should be out of their case and around your neck.

Essentials

- Notebook and pencil with lined and plain paper – write down or draw what you see and where. It will help to identify it later. Mark its cover with centimetres for use as a ruler. You can also use the white paper to reflect light onto a subject or isolate it from a background when taking its picture.

- Hand lens or bug box – you can look through the wrong end of binoculars close up as an emergency magnifier, but a proper one will be better. The type of bug box with a magnifying lid on lets you get a close view without an insect escaping.

- A couple of plastic bags – to use as a seat on damp ground, but mainly for collecting interesting things (although not live animals!). Freezer bags are strong, see-through, have useful twisted wire closures and a space to write on.

- Pooter – the perfect insect collector (see page 101 for how to make one).

- Camera – a phone camera may be enough, especially with a good zoom. You may choose to add a small tripod (such as a gorillapod).

Try to carry a few essentials, including notebook and pencil and a magnifying glass.

- Binoculars – beg, borrow or buy them, but binoculars aren't just for birdwatching. A good pair will fit your eyes well, focus closely enough to use for spotting insects and just make your wildlife watching so much better. Always try them before you buy.

- Collecting tubes – for picking up seeds, small insects or anything else that looks interesting.

- Small paint brush – for moving minibeasts without hurting them.

- Rubber gloves – to pick up anything you don't fancy touching with your hands.

- Field guides – or a smartphone full of apps – to identify what you see.

- String – 5m of strong string, for tying things together. You could also tie knots in it to measure larger objects.

- Cereal bar – emergency rations for hungry naturalists.

Other useful items

- Telescopic inspection mirror – for looking under things, such as ledges in rockpools, or under the caps of fungi without picking them; on top of things you can't reach or for reflecting light onto your subject.

- Torch – it's always useful to carry a small and powerful one with you.

- Tray or a pale umbrella – to catch insects in after you have beaten branches.

- Tweezers – for picking things apart, such as pellets, or picking up tiny objects like seeds.

- Sticky tape – for attaching hairs, seeds or other finds to a page of your notebook – though not live animals!

- Small paper envelopes – for collecting seeds.

- Polarising sunglasses – for reducing reflections when watching fish and rock-pooling.

- Sun cream – especially for the back of your neck if you are spending time on your hands and knees looking at ground life.

- Pocket microscope – if you want to look at the world in detail.

- Bat detector – for bats, but also good for grasshoppers and crickets.

- Plastic spoon – for singling out pond creatures in a collecting tray.

- Sandwich box – for sandwiches, of course, but good protection for anything delicate you collect.

- Pencils – take two sharpened ones and you probably won't need a sharpener with you. Using crayons is one of the quickest ways of drawing things you can't bring home.

- Watercolour kit – a small, lightweight kit with just a few colours. One small brush will be enough.

- Water bottle (with water) – not just to drink or for your watercolours, but a bit of water can soften a dragonfly skin to make its joints move again, can encourage a sleeping slug or snail to reveal itself and can make the colours of pebbles come alive.

- OS map – to show where the best wildlife features are likely to be.

- Smartphone – for emergencies, reference and apps and maps.

- Seed for tame birds – you'll get a better look at ducks if they come close to feed.

- Sweep net – for butterflies, but also for sweeping beetles and spiders out of long grass.

A sweep net can catch flying insects as well as those sitting on wildflowers.

The naturalist's bedroom

You don't have to stop watching wildlife just because you have come home, so see how much of this you can get into your home biology lab. Your parents may call it your bedroom, but you'll soon have other ideas!

- Computer and scanner

- Nature table

- Microscope

- Collapsible insect-rearing cages

- Television

- Plants growing and drying

- Telescope

- Tripod

- Bookshelf full of field guides

- Old fish tank for temporarily housing creatures that you want to have a closer look at. Try to make it feel like the wild, with a bit of soil, a few plants and perhaps a water dish.

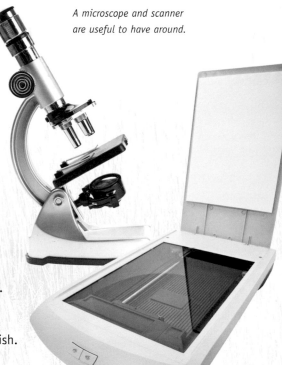

A microscope and scanner are useful to have around.

The naturalist's wardrobe

There's no naturalist style guide, but it's good to have a few of these in your wardrobe:

- Hat with a peak – to shade the sky, stop twigs poking your eyes at night and to keep the rain and sun off.

- Footwear to cope with a range of terrain.

- Coat with pockets so you don't have to carry a bag everywhere.

- Quiet, warm, rustle-free clothing in dark colours.

- You don't need to wear full camouflage unless you want to hide from other wildlife watchers!

- And remember to have something bright to put on if you are crossing roads at night. Remaining hidden from deer and badgers at night is fun. Remaining hidden from drivers is dangerous.

Dark clothing will make it less likely that wildlife will see you.

The naturalist's year

Spring

Spring starts in the warmer south and west and slowly moves north and east at around 0.5-1 mph across the 600 miles from Land's End to John O'Groats. This means that March is a spring month in south-west England, but April is still a winter month in much of Scotland. Spring won't reach the far north until May.

In any one place, though, spring is usually our briefest season. It is marked by the first flush of catkins on the trees, primroses and bluebells in the woods, the arrival of thousands of nesting seabirds on cliffs and islands, butterflies along country lanes and birds singing from every bush and tree.

It is a time of growth, arrivals and departures, and naturalists like to get out and note when all the different events of spring take place. When did you see the first swallow last year? When did you see your first flowering primrose the year before that? Can't remember? Well, spring is the perfect time to start a wildlife diary so that you never forget again.

Watch for frogs heading to ponds to breed.

These dates are so important that a whole science has grown around them. It is called phenology, which is the study of timing in nature. If you keep a spring journal or wildlife diary from now onwards, you will be surprised at how much these dates will change. In the past 40 years, spring has come earlier for plants by around 10 days, for birds by about a week and for insects by about two weeks. Who knows what will happen in the next 40 years?

Look for:

- Singing birds.

- Wildflowers in woodlands and then in the hedgerows.

- The first baby rabbits, foxes and badgers above ground.

- Brimstone, orange-tip and peacock butterflies.

- Frogs, toads and newts heading to the ponds to breed.

- Leaves opening on trees.

- Freshwater fish warming themselves up in the shallows.

Summer is a great time to watch wildlife. The days are long and warm. This not only gives you plenty of time for looking, but also means that some of the night creatures have to venture out in daylight to find enough food.

A lot of wildlife, from flowers to dragonflies, can only be seen in the summer months. And even then, some things only come out when it's sunny. For example, don't bother looking for most blue butterflies unless the summer sun is shining.

Reptiles, amphibians, bats and dormice will be active, if still hard to see. And thousands of migrant birds will be taking advantage of the long feeding days to nest here.

In later summer, many of the birds will hide away to replace their worn-out feathers in private. Many birdwatchers then turn their attentions to other wildlife – orchids, moths, butterflies, dragonflies, hoverflies or bats, for example.

We tend to think of the summer as being at least June, July and August, but some big autumn events may happen in those months. By mid-July most seabirds will have left their nesting cliffs, cuckoos will have gone and by the end of August all of our swifts will already have left for Africa.

Most wildflowers have finished blooming before the end of June, and some hedgerow fruits are ripe before the end of August. Perhaps we are better off not thinking too much about what we call the season!

Look for:

- Seabirds on their cliffs.

- Dragonflies and damselflies on every pond, lake and river.

- Listen for the squeaky calls of baby birds and watch them being fed by their parents.

- Caterpillars under nettle leaves and on ragwort plants.

- Bats on warm summer evenings.

Look out for puffins on cliffs.

17

Autumn

When does summer turn into autumn? Sooner than you think, and certainly sooner for some wildlife than for others. If waders have failed to breed in the High Arctic, some may start south on their 'autumn migration' as early as late June. Then again, in mild years, some trees may still have leaves as late as December. In other words, autumn is a season determined by what is happening in nature itself, rather than the date on a human calendar.

Autumn is a time to prepare for the hard winter to come, but it is also the time to cash in on all the summer growth. At the same time as there are more young birds and animals around that need food, there are also more seeds and fruits (and young animals) for them to eat. This means that as the temperatures start to fall and the nights start to draw in, the natural world becomes an even more exciting place for a naturalist.

Autumn is horse chestnut time.

Look for:

- Fruits, nuts and seeds in woods and hedgerows.

- Squirrels and jays collecting acorns for the winter.

- Swallows and martins gathering on wires before migrating south.

- More toadstools in any habitat.

- Special moths with fantastic names that only come out in autumn, such as the rosy rustic or merveille du jour.

- Groups of birdwatchers all peering intently – it is the season of rare migrant birds and their dedicated followers!

Whether it's damp, grey and miserable, bright and frosty, or icy and snowy, winter has two characteristics that affect your life as a naturalist and wildlife's fight for survival: it is cold and the days are short.

However cold we may think it is, winters in the UK are warmer than in much of mainland Europe, so we are the winter destination of choice for thousands of birds: whooper and Bewick's swans, pink-footed, brent and barnacle geese and thousands of ducks and wading birds head for our coasts and wetlands to spend the winter.

Smaller birds, especially tits, starlings, finches and buntings, flock together in winter to feed as well. So winter is a great time to see lots of birds.

Look for:

- Deciduous woodlands – the shapes of bare trees without leaves can be easier to see.

- Animal tracks.

- Nests, squirrel dreys and witches' brooms (a disease) in bare trees.

- Occasional moths.

- Fungi.

Bullfinches are quite shy, so it is easier to see them in a tree without leaves.

School holidays

Birdwatchers can get a bit frustrated that the most exciting and unpredictable times – the spring migration, the breeding season and the autumn migration – all mainly happen during the school term. You can still see plenty of birds in the school holidays, but if your interests are wider than that, you can fit lots of wildlife watching into your holidays.

Summer holiday: the best time for butterflies and moths, dragonflies, upland flowers, reptiles.

Autumn half term: look for wildfowl migrating and geese streaming into our wetlands. Search the woodlands, sand dunes, hedgerows and heathlands for fungi. Look for hedgerow trees full of fruit, and keep an eye on them over the winter to see which birds and mammals are scoffing the lot!

Christmas holidays: fieldfares and redwings will be all over the fields, and a light sprinkling of snow is great for showing up animal tracks. Some of our trees are easy to identify without their summer leaves. Identify and remember what they are in winter – as they will be the same species in the same place in the summer!

February half term: in southern England, you may see the first signs of spring. Wherever you live, now is the time to start learning birdsong, because there won't be many species singing. Get to know them now and you will be ready to learn the new arrivals later in the spring.

Easter holidays: often the best time for early flowers, migrant birds, the first butterflies, baby rabbits.

Spring half term: if you are not stuck indoors revising for exams, spend the whole of this week out watching nature! It's the best time, with bluebells, badger cubs, the magnificent dawn chorus of bird song, newts in the ponds and all sorts of life bursting from every tree and bush. Get out there now!

Get out to see the bluebells in spring half term.

Wildlife obviously exists all the time, but you will have your best chance of seeing it if you know when it is most active. In general, dawn and dusk are the best times, but not for everything. Butterflies and dragonflies need the warmth of the sun to be really active, and some flowers only open in the middle of the day.

Even most of the animals we think of as nocturnal come out at dusk. Tawny owls and some bats wait until it is really dark, but even so you can sometimes surprise them at the other end of the night.

In the spring and summer, most birds will be active from dawn for a few hours. They may stop moving about altogether by around 10am, so prepare for early starts. At least once in June or early in your summer holidays, try to get up and out before dawn – you will be amazed at how different the world of wildlife is before most people get up.

Some creatures, such as snakes and lizards, need to warm up before they can move about and feed. You can sometimes see them basking in early morning sunshine. Later in the day, they will move too fast to spot.

Most moths and a lot of other insects come out only at night, but not all of them. There are more day-flying moths than butterflies in the UK.

Remember that some habitats become much more dangerous after dark, such as woodlands where twigs can poke at your eyes, or the coast where the tide can creep up behind you. Be careful. You need to be watching at the best time for wildlife watchers as well as for the wildlife itself.

A grass snake takes an early morning sunbathe.

Weather watch

Without rain and all the other different sorts of weather we get in the UK, we wouldn't have such a wide range of wildlife to enjoy. Here are some tips about what to look for in different kinds of weather.

Rain

Look for slugs, snails, frogs and toads on the wet ground, and watch for pigeons and jackdaws lifting their wings on rooftops to wash their wing-pits! Don't look for ducks, bats or butterflies because they will either be sheltering or not looking their best.

Snails are attracted to the wet ground.

Cloudy days

Birds are often more active for longer on cloudy mornings, and they are easier to see high in the trees than against a bright blue sky. The lack of deep shadows can also help when trying to spot deer under trees. Some pale flowers look better out of the sunshine.

Colours of flowers or flying birds may look very different on a cloudy day.

Snow

Look for animal tracks after snow, but also look for newly arrived birds that have come in to avoid bad weather. In the right places, with the right luck, you may spot a white mountain hare or even a white stoat.

Look out for bird tracks in the snow.

Bright sunshine

Butterflies, dragonflies and other insects will only be really active in sunny weather. Sunlight shining into water helps you spot fish below the surface. Don't forget that some flowers open only in the sunshine.

Wind

Birdwatchers pray for onshore winds, especially autumn winds from the east. These will bring birds closer to shore to be seen and migrant birds and insects will blow in from Europe and Asia. Strong westerly winds blowing right across the Atlantic Ocean can even bring rare birds and butterflies here from America. That's 2,000 miles over the ocean, without landing once. Other wildlife may avoid the wind, but it can help you get closer to some animals if the wind is blowing your human scent away.

Fog

You may not be able to see much in fog, but when you do, you can often get quite close to it. Sound can travel well in fog and mist, but wildlife can often look much bigger in the gloom. Don't be fooled into thinking that Tibbles the cat is a mystery black panther!

Sound travels well on a foggy day like this.

Site guide

You can find wildlife anywhere, but there are real hot spots, with special creatures, huge numbers or easy viewing. Many are nature reserves, looked after for wildlife and wildlife watchers alike, but some are simply stunning places to be. Visit as many as you can. In general, head north and west for big numbers, and south and east for more variety.

Top places for:

- Marine nature reserves – Lundy Island (1), St Abbs Head (2), Kimmeridge Bay (3)

- Seabird colonies – Bass Rock (4), Farne Islands (5), Skomer (6), Rathlin Island (7), Isles of Scilly (8)

- Mountain and moorlands wildlife – the Cairngorms (9)

- Wildflowers – Malham Tarn (10), Old Winchester Hill (11), The Outer Hebrides (12)

- Red kites, as well as lots of other wildlife – Gigrin Farm (13), Welsh oak woodlands (14)

- Fantastic wetlands – Titchwell (15), Wicken Fen (16), Leighton Moss (17), Minsmere (18)

- Great wildlife spots – New Forest (19), North Norfolk (20), Minsmere (18), Wicken Fen (16), Isles of Scilly (8), Shetland (27)

- Wader flocks – Snettisham (21), Morecambe Bay (22)

- White-tailed eagles, divers, otters – Isle of Mull (23)

- Wildfowl – Slimbridge (24), Caerlaverock (25), Welney (26)

Thousands of wading birds live on Morecambe Bay.

Patch work

The UK has lots of wildlife because our land is so varied and is used in so many different ways: including farmland for crops and animals, woodlands, mountains, lakes and rivers, the coast, heathlands and many more. As a wildlife watcher, you can only ever hope to get to know a small part of it really well. And if you want to compare wildlife between seasons and years, you will need to focus on somewhere that you can go regularly and learn about – we call this area your 'local patch'.

What does a good local patch need?

- Easy regular access in all weathers.

- Water – whether it's a canal, river, reservoir or a sea bay, you find more wildlife near water.

- Trees – the more different types and the older the better.

- Not too many people, especially dog-walkers. You won't see much wildlife if dogs scare it away.

- Good places to watch from.

- Somewhere you like going – although once you start spotting wildlife you will like it anyway!

- Open, sunny areas, such as a south-facing grassy bank, where flowers will grow and insects will warm themselves up.

- A good route around it.

- To be safe – watching wildlife is exciting enough without putting yourself in danger.

Get to know your local patch by going there regularly.

Finding your patch

Ordnance Survey maps and Google satellite maps are a great way to start looking for your perfect local patch. See if you can work out a route that takes you through several different habitats. You may need to ask permission to go to some places, and you will need to let your parent or guardian know where you are going, but there is nothing like having a regular circuit that you know well.

Even if you live in the middle of a city, there will be places you can go.

Local canals and waterways can often be used as your patch.

Making tracks

The term 'tracks' can mean two things. It's the path a creature takes when it is going about its daily business, or the foot, beak, tail or other prints it leaves behind. A common way to find the path an animal takes is by seeing where it leaves its footprints. But be aware, many animals don't take fixed routes, so they will leave footprint tracks all over the place.

Rabbits, badgers and deer all tread pathways so regularly that they form tracks. Even without footprints, you can often tell what creature made them. Badgers, for example, almost always go under obstacles in their way. Deer and rabbits jump over them. So if you see a woodland path that goes under a fallen branch without any plants growing through it, you have probably found a badger track.

Some animals leave a trail that you can smell. Foxes and grass snakes both leave strong, sharp smells that are rarely forgotten. And sometimes you will find the animal at the end of its track – a slug on its silvery trail or the winkle creeping across the bottom of a sandy rockpool.

When you find a footprint, count its toes. Are there claw marks or foot pads? Is there a line where a tail has been dragged through behind the feet? Tracks can tell you what the creature was doing. Tracks made by a running animal will not only be deeper but differently spaced from those made while just ambling about.

Tracks can also tell you how long ago an animal passed through a place, or whether a hole is being lived in. Sprinkle a bit of damp sand in front of a hole and come back the next day to see if there are new tracks in it. If so, someone's at home.

Track tips

- Count the number of toes, claws and webs on tracks you find. Badgers have five toes with long claws, for example, and some birds don't have a rear claw.

- Look for different shapes of front and back foot tracks.

- Look along the lower strand of barbed wire fences, for animal hair. Badger hair has three colour bands; fox hair is red, and deer hair is hollow and stiff.

- Look at any bunches of feathers you find. If a fox catches a bird, it will bite through the feathers; if a sparrowhawk is the killer, it will pluck the feathers so they will be whole.

- Look under any leaves with holes in. You may find a happy vegetarian.

Poo and other waste

Animal poo and bird sick may not sound lovely, but they are useful for wildlife watchers. They can tell you what wildlife is in the area, how many there are, where to find them and what they have been eating.

If you find animal poo, it means the animal in question was there not too long ago. If you hadn't thought of looking for it there, that will be helpful. Some animals always poo in the same place, so that will tell you exactly where to find them. Badgers have family toilets called latrines, and woodpigeons and other birds may sleep and poo in the same place for several nights in a row, so if you find a pile, step aside and look up!

Some animals send messages with their poo: this is my place! So if you find it somewhere very obvious, such as on a river bank stone, it's an animal staking a claim. Very smelly poo may contain chemical signals to rivals or potential mates.

Pellets

Many hunting birds sick up pellets of fur, bones, insect shells and other indigestible material. Owl pellets are the most well known, but kestrels, herons, and even crows will produce pellets too.

Taking pellets apart is a great way not only to find what an owl has been eating but also to discover what small creatures are found in the area. Skulls of mice, voles, shrews and small birds remain whole in pellets and are easy to identify. Soak the pellet in a bit of disinfectant and you can then tease it apart with cocktail sticks or tweezers to see what was on the menu!

Poo facts

- If it has white in it you have probably found bird poo.

- Small piles of poo are usually left by plant eaters such as rabbits and deer.

- Bat poo in roofs dries out and is completely harmless and not smelly. It can even help insulate the roof.

- Insect poo is called frass.

- Predators have the smelliest poo!

Why not make a skull collection from pellets?

Holes and homes

Most animals don't think of homes in the way that we do, as bases from which to explore our world and return to for safety. Some do, such as badgers, rabbits, some spiders, crabs and even snakes. But more often, creatures only use them for one purpose – raising a family or sleeping – and they may move around a lot. Other creatures don't build a 'home', but return to the same place to rest, like limpets which return to the same piece of rock at low tide after spending the high tide under water eating algae.

Classic holes

- Mining and mason bee holes: less than 1cm across, and dug into sandy soil or soft walls, usually south-facing.

- Razor shell holes: a small hole low down on a sandy beach just above the sea may have a 25cm razor shell living in it.

- Vole holes: 2-3cm holes in grass may lead into vole tunnels.

- Rabbit holes: up to around 15cm in diameter and usually built into a hedgebank or woodland edge, perhaps under a bramble bush – there are likely to be several together.

- Fox earth: a single hole that is usually taller than it is wide, perhaps 15x25cm or bigger. Dug deeper into the ground than a rabbit burrow, so with a bigger spoil heap. Often with scraps of bone or other food around. Can smell sharp.

- Badger sett: a group of large holes, wider than tall, each with a large spoil heap and possibly straw bedding by the entrance. Paths connect these holes to outlying ones.

A fox cub by its earth.

- Kingfisher and sand martin holes: dug into soft river banks or sandy quarryside. Martins nest together in colonies.

- Brown hare's form: slight dips in the ground on a field track may be where a brown hare sleeps for the day.

- Squirrel's drey: a large untidy bundle of leaves and twigs high up in a tree.

- Harvest mouse's nest: a tightly woven ball of grass about the size of a tennis ball in rough grass or attached to reeds.

- Magpie's nest: a big single ball-shaped nest of twigs high in a tree.

- Rookery: where rooks breed together in groups. Lots of big untidy nests together high in trees.

A squirrel's drey.

A kingfisher enters its nest hole.

Bringing wildlife to you

Wildlife has simple needs – food, water, the right climate, somewhere safe from predators and safe to raise a family. Together, we call these things a 'niche'.

Every plant or animal has a slightly different niche, but many overlap. You may find plantains and dandelions growing on a grass verge, for example, but the plantains will be on or right next to the footpath because they are better at coping with being trodden on. They have tougher leaves that spread out close to the ground. We call this adaptation. Every plant or animal is adapted to live in its own niche.

Using niches

When you start to recognise the different niches, you can start to work them to your advantage. Birds need food and somewhere to nest, so by feeding them and putting nestboxes up somewhere where you can observe them in secret (such as your garden) you will bring them in.

Many wildflowers need poor soil and don't like mowing, so by leaving part of a lawn uncut and unfed, you may find wildflowers start to grow – and you can always add seeds. And once you have your wildflowers, you will start seeing more insects coming to feed on them.

Bumblebees and mining bees may need nest holes, hedgehogs may want somewhere to spend the winter, and pond life will need a pond!

Wildflowers will attract insects.

Tips for attracting wildlife

- Try making squeaking noises by kissing the back of your hand loudly. This can bring small birds out of bushes (birdwatchers call this technique 'pishing').

- Squeak loudly through pursed lips to a barn owl and it may come to investigate you.

- Hoot at tawny or little owls and they may hoot back – and sometimes come to frighten you away, so be careful.

- Squeak at weasels, stoats and mink and they come to investigate because it probably sounds like an injured animal – an easy meal.

- Squeak at rabbits and they will run away – they don't want to be near what sounds like an easy meal!

- Push twigs or small branches into the mud at the edges of ponds for dragonflies to perch on – it can work for kingfishers, too.

- Leave a bathroom light on and its window open on summer evenings to attract moths and lacewings in (it's easier to catch a moth in a bathroom than in the clutter of your bedroom).

- In March, knock on the base of a big tree in a wood with a stick. A woodpecker may come to have a look at you.

- Make your own window hide – cover part of a window but leave eye holes. Then put a bird feeder just outside so you can have a good look.

- Make your own garden hide – an old sheet or netting over a garden chair will do – just so you can see out and wildlife doesn't think you look like a human.

- In dry places, provide water for drinking and bathing.

- Make a pond – the bigger the better.

Build a pond and wildlife will find it before long!

Wildlife gardening

If we could put all our gardens together, they would be bigger than the combined area of our national nature reserves. So if we could make them all better for wildlife that would be brilliant. Most gardens are a bit like the edges of woodlands, so it's not surprising that a lot of garden wildlife also lives in woods. That's obvious for birds, hedgehogs and butterflies, but it also goes for many other insects.

The more countryside features we can include in our gardens the better they are for wildlife, and the more of it you will be able to see, however big or small your garden. Even a city window box will attract bees and hoverflies.

If bats pass through your garden, they may like a bat box.

- Make a wildlife pond – even a small, temporary pond will fill with wildlife. If you can make a permanent pond, make it at least 50cm deep to stop it freezing solid in winter. Plant it with native pond plants (garden centres should know which ones will be suitable), and don't put fish in it.

- Make a compost heap – it will fill up with insects, centipedes, worms and snails, and if you are really lucky, a hedgehog or grass snake may choose to nest in it.

- Make a log pile – take logs of at least 10cm diameter and stack them up in the corner of your garden – it will soon be colonised by spiders, beetles and woodlice among other things. That will then attract wrens.

A log pile makes a perfect home for beetles and woodlice.

- Place a few flat sheets of metal, plastic or roofing felt down and leave them in place. Check underneath them once a week and see what has come to shelter there or warm up. You could find anything from an ant nest to slow-worms or a family of voles or shrews. But slugs, earwigs and centipedes are more likely.

- Plant insect-friendly plants – these can be wildflowers, but older varieties of garden flowers are also good sources of nectar for butterflies and bees. Many insects will need different plants in their younger stages – especially nettles and other wild plants.

  - Leave a strip of lawn to grow taller and plant meadow plants in there. Leave them long enough to set their seeds, but mow it in July or August when the seeds have ripened and fallen off.

  - Don't be too tidy – seed heads and dead plants are often food for birds in their own right, but may also house insects, from earwigs to ladybirds.

  - Put up nestboxes for birds and bees and roosting boxes for bats and hedgehogs.

Let a bit of your lawn grow wild.

Widening your interest

Watching wildlife is a great activity because you can do it on your own, with one or two friends, or in much bigger groups. You can also combine it with other activities to increase your wildlife watching time.
If you are waiting to bat at a school rounders game, can you count the swifts flying over, hear skylarks or count bumblebees on the clover?

Spread the word

If you do any of these things, then it's really good to tell people about them. Spotting and counting wildlife is really important in nature conservation. We have to know what's out there to decide if it needs any help – so wildlife watchers are always doing surveys. And it's people like you, enjoying wildlife for its own sake, who are the foundation of it all.

There is no end to the amount of wildlife that people would like you to look out for: birds, bats, basking sharks, butterflies and moths, dormice, jellyfish, glow worms and sulphur tuft, to name a few. In short, if you look for something, someone will want to know about it, whether you have found it or not.

Sharing what you learn in nature can help to protect it.

A group of friends who watch wildlife will never be bored!

Get involved

Some of the groups that regularly ask for volunteer surveyors include the RSPB, BTO, Plantlife, The Mammal Society, BugLife, Butterfly Conservation, Woodland Trust and local Wildlife Trusts. You often only need to identify one species to take part, and you would be told just what to do.

Buglife - www.buglife.org.uk

Ispot - www.ispot.org.uk

Natural History Museum - www.nhm.ac.uk

Plantlife - www.plantlife.org.uk

The RSPB - www.rspb.org.uk

The Wildlife Trusts - www.wildlifetrusts.org

Woodland Trust - www.woodlandtrust.org.uk

Habitats

The word 'habitat' means the type of place where an animal or plant normally lives. Woodlands, lakes and gardens are all habitats.

However, usually we will need to go into more detail than that. We may talk about oak woodland, which will have mainly oak trees, but will have plenty of other plants growing there as well. We may make sure we mention if it's a shallow or deep lake because they are likely to have different animals living in them – you won't find many diving ducks on a lake that would be shallow enough for a swan to reach the plants on the bottom. And gardens can be very different types of habitat depending on how they are looked after and where they are.

Remember though, animals and plants can view their own habitats very differently to us. A caterpillar munching away on an oak leaf in a garden may be just as happy as if it were in an ancient woodland. To that caterpillar, one oak tree is a habitat all of its own!

Specialist or generalist?

Some animals and plants are only found in one habitat. You won't find a limpet away from seashore rocks, for example. These animals and plants are called 'specialists'. You can find others in all sorts of places. Wrens or foxes will live on heathlands, upland moors, gardens, woodlands and even on the seashore. We call these 'generalists'. You, as a human being, are the ultimate generalist! People get everywhere.

And something as big as an eagle may live in a huge area that covers bare mountain tops, heather moorland and even down into woodland. Even if the eagle doesn't need the woodland, some of its prey, such as red deer, may.

A limpet is a specialist.

This buff-tip caterpillar lives on oak leaves, but it doesn't mind where the tree is!

Scale

All this means that you have to think about the scale when thinking about habitats, and that will help you to see more wildlife. If you are interested in millipedes, for example, it's no use going to a woodland and wandering around hoping to spot one. You need to know that they like to live under logs and stones in damp places. That may be in a woodland, but there are other places where a suitable millipede habitat may be found, such as in your own garden.

Some of the smallest habitats, such as under a rock, are the least noticed and are unspoiled, so be especially careful when investigating that you don't upset what lives there.

What would you find living in this habitat?

Cliffs

Cliffs are fantastic but often dangerous places – for both people and wildlife. Many birds choose to nest on cliffs because they are so hard for predators to get to, and it is easy to take off from a cliff. This also makes them one of the country's most unspoilt habitats, but not always the oldest. The famous white chalk cliffs of Dover stay white because of frequent rock falls. Before plants have a chance to grow on the cliff face, it crumbles away, revealing more fresh clean chalk.

Sea cliffs are not only great places to spot the wildlife that lives on the cliffs, but also good places to watch for wildlife out at sea. Not only can you see farther out to sea from a high place, but you can also look into the dips and troughs of the waves that may hide passing ducks or dolphins from beach watchers. Some people spend hours watching the sea from cliff tops. It's not for everyone, but these seawatchers spot wildlife that no one else ever sees.

Don't forget that some rocks are also great for fossils, so beaches below the cliffs are good places to look for these, especially after fresh rock falls from the winter storms. Pay attention to any safety notices though.

On the cliff

Cliffs often have interesting plants and lichens growing on them, but you will need binoculars to get a good look at the best ones because they will be out of reach.

As well as the seabirds that nest on cliffs, this habitat is great for the world's fastest bird, the peregrine falcon. These fabulous birds swoop down over the rocks after an unsuspecting pigeon or jackdaw, and are so well-adapted to cliffs that they can be found in many man-made inland cliff sites. Man-made cliffs? You know them as skyscrapers or cathedrals in our towns and cities.

The white cliffs of Dover are made of crumbly chalk.

Rocky coasts, with their mix of sandy bays, rocky outcrops and rockpools, are fantastic places for wildlife. Even before you delve into the rockpools themselves, you will see how the wildlife positions itself in relation to the sea. At the very top of the beach, where there may be the occasional bit of salt spray from the waves, you may find sea-pink flowers and there will be different lichens on the rocks at the top of the beach than there are a bit lower down.

Farther down you will find the first of the shells, probably barnacles and a few periwinkles. Lower still there will be topshells and mussels, but all of these need to be covered by the tide occasionally because they only feed when they are covered with water. And at the bottom of the beach, only exposed at the lowest tides, you may see jelly-like blobs on the rocks. These are sea anemones.

Rockpools

This is the rockpool zone. There will be a mix of creatures that always live there and others that get trapped by each tide. Almost the whole community can change twice a day as the tide ebbs and flows.

When it comes to looking in the pools themselves, the same applies as for ponds – try to keep still and let the wildlife come out – and wear polarising sunglasses to cut out reflections. The rockpool residents, especially some of the shore crabs and larger shannies, will usually have a favourite ledge or stone to hide under. If you disturb them with your pond net, it is kindest to put them back where you found them.

When looking in rockpools, try to keep your shadow off the water.

Sandy beaches

Everyone loves a sandy beach, but they can often seem a bit lifeless for wildlife. Shingle beaches may look even worse. There are several reasons for this: sandy beaches are often crowded with people who accidentally frighten the wildlife away; much of it stays hidden under the sand until the tide comes in; and there really isn't as much to see on a sandy beach as on a rocky one.

The sand on our sandy beaches is made from rocks and pebbles, ground up by the tide. (In tropical countries, the white sand is made from ground-up coral and parrotfish poo!)

Sandy beach tips

A worm cast from a ragworm.

- Try to get there early, before other people have scared off the birds. You may see wading birds along the edge of the sea, and gulls bobbing about just off shore.

- Look along the tideline carefully. There will be interesting dead things washed up, but also living creatures, from sandhoppers and sea slaters to rock pipits and common shrews.

- If there is anyone digging for fishing bait down at the water's edge, ask if you can see what they have dug up – lugworms and ragworms are fascinating in their own right.

- Some beaches may have seals on – don't approach too close if you find one.

- Spend a bit of time looking at the shells that have washed up.

If you see seals, don't disturb them.

Sand dunes

In some places, the sea is washing more and more sand up on to the land. When this happens, sand dunes may form. In time, special plants start to grow on the dunes and this stops the sand from shifting. Marram grass is the most important of these grasses. It's really spiky!

Behind the dunes, wet marshy areas called dune 'slacks' may develop and these can hold amazing wildlife that is found nowhere else.

Sand dunes are great for seeing animal tracks, especially if the sand is wet. Look out for signs of foxes and rabbits and even toads in the slacks.

Sea buckthorn bushes, with their bright orange berries, may hold fieldfares, redwings and other migrant birds, and unusual plants such as sea spurge may live here.

The sandhill rustic moth lives in the dunes, along with wildflowers such as the early gentian. You might find red toadstools in the autumn.

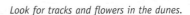

Look for tracks and flowers in the dunes.

Mudflats and estuaries

You may be surprised at how fantastic these grey, muddy places are for wildlife. They are among our last truly wild big habitats. They are places of change – from river freshwater to sea saltwater. And wherever there is change there are opportunities for wildlife to get a foothold.

The biggest estuaries, such as Morecambe Bay in northwest England and The Wash in eastern England, hold thousands of birds all year around. But those birds change almost daily, making these tremendously exciting places for naturalists.

Huge numbers of waders pass through estuaries on their way to or from their breeding grounds. Many others spend the winter on the estuaries along with thousands of ducks and geese.

Estuary treasure

These birds come to feed on the invisible riches of estuaries, which are the millions of tiny worms and shellfish living in the mud and washed in by the tide. Along with heathlands, these are among our most underrated habitats, but not by naturalists.

Estuaries are famous for birds, but they may also hold otters, seals, flatfish, crabs and tonnes of shellfish – remember that bird food may be wildlife, too!

Don't forget to look in the mud for worms and shellfish!

A redshank on an estuary.

44

Shush! Don't tell too many people, but machair ('mak-kair') is one of Scotland's best-kept secrets. Machair is the low strip of fertile ground that forms between the sea and the peat bogs on some Scottish islands. The seashell soil balances the acid from the peat to make a fantastic growing medium for wildflowers. And where there are wildflowers there will also be wild animals.

Most of these Scottish islands don't have ground predators such as stoats, weasels and hedgehogs, so the machair is a safe place for nesting birds such as twites, corncrakes, dunlins and ringed plovers.

The plants are home to exciting insects, such as a bee called the northern colletes, the belted beauty moth and the great yellow bumblebee.

Machair is a great place to see wildflowers.

Lots of wildlife

The rare sand lizard lives in the machair on the island of Coll and otters pass through on their way to the coast. For a few short weeks of summer, the colourful strip of machair flowers is among the best in Europe. It is full of yellow rattle, wild thyme, birds-foot trefoil, harebells and even its own special marsh orchid that is found nowhere else.

Maintaining machair

Machair is so rare partly because it needs the right conditions to grow, but also because it needs people and our grazing animals to keep it in check. As with many other habitats that look completely natural, human influence is important and the small farming and crofting communities that live there can keep it just right.

Saltmarsh

Saltmarshes are flat areas mainly covered by the sea at high tide but revealing a network of muddy creeks and pools as the tide retreats. They can be vital for breeding and wintering wading birds and also have their own special plant life that has to cope with spending some of its time under seawater – being nibbled by fish and crabs – some in the open air and some under rain. Sea lavender and samphire are typical saltmarsh plants, with annual seablite on the slightly higher ground.

The most typical bird on the saltmarsh is the redshank, which loudly warns everything else that you are coming. Saltmarshes can have a surprising number of creatures living there, such as brown hares and lizards, and winter visiting birds such as snow buntings, shore and skylarks and linnets.

Bird life

Saltmarshes are great for wildfowl, including wigeons, teals and brent geese. They are also great places to see birds of prey such as marsh harriers, short-eared owls and even peregrines looking for a duck dinner.

They are not the easiest places to watch wildlife, but a walk along the edge of a saltmarsh as the tide is coming in and pushing wildlife out of the creeks can be very rewarding.

Look out for short-eared owls on a saltmarsh.

The creeks and pools of a saltmarsh attract a lot of wildlife.

The sea around us may look to be all the same – big, wet and cold, but it is really a whole range of habitats that run into one another. Different depths of water and whether the bottom is sandy or rocky, how rough it usually is, how warm it is and how far from land all make a difference to what lives there.

The warm currents called the Gulf Stream that flow up the west coast of Britain and Ireland, keep the water there warmer than in the east. But our strong westerly winds make western seas rougher.

From land, we can sometimes tell what the sea is like by watching the wildlife. If you see a flock of eider ducks, for example, you can be sure there are mussel beds underneath the water, and it is probably less than 10m deep.

There may well be a mussel bed under these eider ducks.

Lakes

Big lakes can often be a bit disappointing for the wildlife watcher. The wildlife is there, but most of it will be under water or staying out in the middle where it feels safe. You are often best looking around the edges, especially if there is any marshy land or reeds growing there.

However, some of our big lakes do have special fish, found nowhere else, and they can have lots of ducks and geese, especially in the winter.

Lake plants

Don't forget to look at the plants growing around and in a big lake. Some of these can be special. Those growing round the edge range from big willows and reeds down to little submerged plants, from flowering plants that keep their leaves submerged but stick their flowers up into the air to attract insects, to algae and mosses.

Many of these have to cope with drying out if the edge of the lake dries up in summer, or trying to get enough light as the water deepens around them. They also have to cope with being buffeted by waves, eaten and trampled by animals and changes in the water caused by pollution, especially farm chemicals washed into the water. It's not an easy life!

Grey herons stand at the edge of a lake.

Canals are usually sections of a river that people have straightened, deepened and slowed down to make them suitable for river traffic. Canals have tow paths that you can walk down, and often provide a bit of greenery in a city. The downside is that the bankside vegetation that would support all sorts of wildlife has usually been cut back, the water is likely to be murky and there may be a lot of other people around putting the wildlife off. It doesn't mean the wildlife isn't there – there will be fish, probably kingfishers and certainly moorhens and dragonflies around.

River life

Rivers are much more variable and much more exciting. Young rivers, high in the hills, will be small, fast-flowing and clear. As they work their way to the sea, they will go through rough and smooth patches, called pools and 'riffles', which hold different wildlife, before becoming wide, slow rivers, with reeds and other bankside vegetation.

The age and speed of the river makes a difference to what wildlife you will see. For example, dippers will be in the faster upper reaches, and kingfishers farther down where the water is clearer. You may find stonefly larvae in the oxygen-rich upper reaches, but more mayflies and damselflies farther down.

Some wildlife, such as salmon and eels, head right up from the sea to high pools. There is always something to see near a river.

Look for dippers in the upper reaches.

Reedbeds

Reedbeds are home to some great creatures. In the summer, you can see sedge warblers in any summer reedbed, and reed warblers in the southern ones, but you could be really lucky and see a bearded tit or even a bittern as well. Marsh harriers may be patrolling overhead, and water rails may be squealing from the reeds.

In early autumn, thousands of swallows and martins flock to reedbeds to spend the night. Even in winter, there will be starlings and reed buntings, and perhaps a barn owl hunting overhead.

But it's not just birds. Reedbeds are important places for water voles, otters, raft spiders, various rare moths, eels, frogs and even harvest mice with their tiny ball nests.

The reeds

Reedbeds are watery places, dominated by mainly one species of plant. You guessed it, the common reed. But drier parts of reedbeds contain more special wildflowers, from hemp agrimony to yellow iris.

The reeds grow to 3m tall and die back every year. The dead reeds don't rot away as quickly as the new ones grow, so they build up. This means that reedbeds are always slowly drying out, making it easier for trees to grow there. Eventually, they would become willow woodland if left on their own. Luckily, most big reedbeds are now looked after for wildlife – and for people to harvest the reeds to make thatched roofs – so as long as we keep supporting wildlife charities, reedbeds and their special wildlife should be safe.

Reeds grow to 3m tall.

Fen, marsh and wetland

Almost all these areas are now nature reserves, and with good reason. Wetlands have more wildlife of a greater range than any other habitat. That's because they have such variety, from willow trees, nettles and iris beds, to rough grassland and reedbed, muddy edges and open water of assorted depths. Just think of all the different animals and plants that can make a home in such places. Some birds will be found nowhere else, such as bitterns, marsh harriers and bearded tits, but others like barn owls or wrens will live here as well as many other places.

A few mammals, like water voles and otters, rely on watery places, but wetlands are also great places for seeing deer and even small mammals such as field voles.

Some insects live in wetlands and nowhere else, such as the Fenn's wainscot moth or the rare swallowtail butterfly. But they are good places to see much more common butterflies too, as well as dragonflies.

Places of change

One of the best things about wetlands is that they are always changing. They attract migrant birds, have a range of wildflowers and insects that are very seasonal and change with the weather, time of day and time of year. You never know exactly what to expect. But if you visit on a quiet day for your chosen type of wildlife, you can usually find something else to enjoy instead.

A swallowtail butterfly can only be seen in wetlands.

Ponds

Garden ponds, farm ponds, village duck ponds – all have wildlife worth looking at. Generally, the bigger, deeper and quieter the pond the more wildlife you will find. The fewer fish the better, too, unless you want to watch the fish themselves.

When you want to investigate a pond, it's really tempting to rush straight up to it with a pond net and see what you can catch. It's much better to sneak up carefully though and to try to have a look first, preferably without appearing on the pond creature's skyline. Then remain still and watch for a while.

You may see birds come to drink or bathe, or mammals coming to drink. You will probably start to see pond skaters on the surface, perhaps also water boatmen or three-tailed mayfly larvae walking along the bottom and even sticklebacks. As soon as you stick a net in, much of this will try to escape, but pond dipping is still one of the best ways to see what's in there.

Keep an eye out for frogs in your local ponds.

Pond dipping
Also works for rockpools, canals, slow rivers and lakes

The most important thing when dipping a pond is to stay safe. So cover up any cuts with a waterproof plaster, be careful not to poke anyone with your net, and, above all, don't fall in!

Before you dip your net in the water, collect a bit of the water in a tray or sandwich box. This is to keep the creatures in while you look at them. They won't want to be out of the water for long, so do this before you put your net in.

Next, sweep the net in long, smooth, slow movements under the water. Take your net out and immediately empty its contents into the tray – before you have tried to look in your dripping net.

Let the water in the tray settle and see what you can see swimming around. You can then catch the creatures in a plastic spoon in the tray.

Finally, empty the tray back into the pond by submerging it, not by pouring from waist height. Think of the headache that your poor creatures will get otherwise!

Try not to cast a shadow on the water.

Mountain and moorland

Big, windswept mountain landscapes are fantastic places, but not always easy for wildlife watchers. There are plenty of special creatures that live in the uplands, but the larger animals can be hard to creep up on because they can see you coming from a long way off.

Even though they can look bleak, mountain habitats include ponds, rivers, bogs, dry moorland, bare rocks and a lot of space. Look at it all in detail to get the best of it, rather than simply admiring the landscape.

Mountain wildlife

Most of the uplands have red deer, and there are mountain hares which turn white in winter on northern uplands. Breeding birds include the merlin, our smallest falcon, and the magnificent golden eagle, as well as nesting golden plovers, curlews, red grouse, hen harriers and ptarmigans, and there will be meadow pipits everywhere.

Mountain insects include the mountain ringlet butterfly, golden-ringed dragonfly and emperor moth, and don't forget to look at the plants.

Red deer can be seen in most upland areas.

Bilberries go by a variety of names that reflect their importance for people. You will also find heather and bracken, and cotton-grass and moor grass, and because the soils are usually rather poor, insectivorous plants that add to their diet by flycatching – look for sticky sundews and butterworts.

Be prepared

The effect of weather on mountain landscapes can be dramatic, and they can be remote places, so never explore these places on your own and without knowing what the weather has in store. It's not unknown for beautiful purple heathers on a clear morning to be covered in snow by the afternoon!

It's not surprising, then, then that much of the wildlife that can move will head downhill or move further south for the winter.

Lowland heath is a special habitat that the UK has more of than anywhere else, but at first sight it can look rather boring. The main plants are gorse and various heathers, but if not managed it quickly fuzzes up with broom, Scots pine and silver birch trees. Much of the special wildlife of lowland heath needs wide open spaces without trees that predators will use as watch points. This means that heathland conservation often involves removing thousands of tree seedlings.

Heathlands are great places for dragonflies and butterflies. All our reptiles live on southern heaths. They are great places for birds such as Dartford warblers, woodlarks, nightjars and hobbies, and may have roe and the introduced sika deer.

Under threat

Lowland heathlands are semi-natural habitats. That means that they have developed over thousands of years of interaction between people, their animals and wildlife. People cleared trees from the areas and then grazed them with sheep or goats. This gradually made heathlands open up and created the right conditions for the special plants and the animals that like to eat them. Because people don't use heathlands for grazing so much these days, the trees are more likely to grow back, which would be bad news for the wildlife that lives there.

Nightjars are just one of the birds you might see here.

Forest

The New Forest in Hampshire in southern England is the biggest area of forest that we have, and it's a fantastic place for people and for wildlife. Forest isn't just another word for a woodland. There are trees, but there are also wide open places, areas of heathland and rivers. To be called a forest, the land area has to be large and have at least one-fifth covered with trees.

Forests can be great for wildlife that may otherwise struggle to fit onto our crowded islands, because this gives them a range of habitats. Birds, including honey buzzards, redstarts and wood warblers, depend on forested areas. Forests were originally places for hunting deer, and various species of deer still live here, including red and fallow.

Forests are great places for fungi, from the rare and much sought-after truffles to the fly agaric. And with this range of different habitats within a forest, there is no end to the number of insects you can find in the summer, day or night.

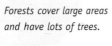
Forests cover large areas and have lots of trees.

A fallow deer.

Woodland edges give wildlife watchers the best of both worlds. The edges of habitats are often the best bits, and can be easier to watch than the middle of a thick woodland. Many creatures move between one habitat and another. For example, rabbits and buzzards may both feed in the open but retreat to woodland edges to sleep. Hedgehogs, badgers and foxes may also come out of the woodland to feed before heading back to the shelter of woodlands during the day.

Badgers usually come out of woodland at night.

A lighter place

The edges of woodlands can also be more interesting for plants and insects because they get more light than farther into the wood. You can often notice that woodland flowers are richer and flower earlier around the edges than in the middle. Plants such as red campion and cuckoo pint will often be nearer the edges.

The edges of older woodlands were often hedges planted to keep farm animals out of the wood (or sometimes in). This means you may find hedgerow trees such as hawthorn or spindle more at the edge of the woodland than inside. It also means the edges may be bushier, so you may be able to find garden warblers, blackcaps, and lesser whitethroats here more than in the middle.

Coniferous woodland

Most coniferous woodland is dense plantations for timber, often too closely packed for light to reach the ground. However, there are a few remnants of the original native pinewoods of Scotland. These have their own special wildlife, from twin-flowers to crested tits and red squirrels.

If the only conifer woods you find are densely planted, you can still find some wildlife. Look for the thinner areas, and look along paths and tracks. There are likely to be coal tits and goldcrests in the treetops and, if you are really lucky, crossbills.

On the ground, look for big living heaps of pine needles. These will be wood ant nests. You will see trails of ants going to and fro, possibly carrying caterpillars or other insect food.

The youngest areas of pines and the clearfell areas where the trees have been recently harvested can be some of the best places for wildlife – short-eared owls and roe deer in the clear fell and tree pipits, woodlarks and adders in the bare areas. On summer evenings, look for nightjars, woodcocks and glow-worms.

Look for red squirrels in the north.

Many pinewoods are too thick and dark to allow much wildlife to live there.

Thousands of years ago, most of the country was covered in woodland, especially oak and beech trees. Most of this was cleared away in the Bronze Age – can you imagine cutting down a huge tree with an axe you have made from stone with an antler handle? A few old pieces of woodland haven't been cut down for at least 400 years. We call these ancient woodlands and they are some of the best places in the UK for wildlife.

Woodland birds, such as woodpeckers, treecreepers and tawny owls live here, but so do dormice, roe deer, speckled wood butterflies, bluebells, primroses and King Alfred's cake fungi.

Newer woodland

Woodland that has been cut down at some point but then has been allowed to grow again can still be great for wildlife. You can often tell this sort of woodland because all the big trees may look to be about the same size and thickness. They may have been replanted 100 years ago after the old woodland had been removed to use as timber in World War 1.

Tawny owls and great spotted woodpeckers both live in woodland.

Meadow, pasture and downland

Don't be fooled into thinking that all open grass fields are the same. In general, the oldest ones that have had the least fertiliser put on them and have had just the right number of animals grazing them are the best. These are the downlands and wildflower meadows. In June they can be alive with butterflies, orchids and beetles.

Greener grassland that has had more grazing may still have wildlife, especially in neglected corners, but is likely to be poorer – the greener the grass, the fewer species it is likely to hold.

Grassland animals

The pyramidal orchid is a favourite with the day-flying burnet moth.

Cows and sheep graze on grasslands. They can attract their own wildlife. Look for magpies trying to steal wool from sheep's backs to line their nests. Or swallows flying around cows looking for flies. Watch for wagtails and starlings grabbing insects that have been disturbed as the cows walk about.

You may also see brown hares in the fields – the larger the field the better for them – but not for other wildlife.

Grazing cattle attract their own wildlife!

Arable farmland

This is land that is used for growing plant crops for people to eat or to feed to farm animals. Crops include wheat and barley, oil seed rape and field beans, sugar-beet, potatoes, carrots and plenty of others. These fields may be surrounded by hedges or fences and come in lots of different sizes.

In general, smaller fields are better for wildlife, especially if there are lots of different types of crop planted next to one another. Bigger fields also often contain only the crop, and no seed-filled weeds or insects for wildlife to eat.

Out in the open

Some species cling to the edges of fields, but others prefer the open spaces so that they can see predators coming. Skylarks, for example, like to nest in the middle of fields. When the crop has grown tall, it's often hard to spot much wildlife in it, but as the crop starts to grow or just after it has been harvested you may have more luck.

Look for partridges and pheasants in fields and kestrels hovering overhead. Rooks, jackdaws and gulls favour ploughed fields. Rabbits can be found around the edges, and brown hares in the middle of the field. Deer or foxes can also often be seen passing through.

On the edge

Sometimes you will find a wildlife-rich strip around the edge of the field. This may be a home for beetles, skipper butterflies and wildflowers.

Skylarks are among the few species that like big fields.

Hedgerows

In most cases, garden hedges are planted from just one type of bush. However, hedges in the countryside tend to be much more interesting. Some countryside hedges are among the oldest features in a landscape, especially if they form a boundary between two landowners. And the older, taller and thicker they are, the better they are for wildlife.

To work out roughly how old a countryside hedge is, count the number of tree species in about 30 big paces and multiply by 100. If the hedge contains mainly hawthorn, it was probably planted in the 18th or early 19th century.

Some hedges are so old that they are just thin strips of ancient woodland. These can have fascinating flowers, including bluebells and Solomon's seal, along with climbers such as honeysuckle and old-man's beard. Look out for fruit trees such as damsons and crab apples here too.

Wildlife-friendly

All these plants mean that hedges can be great for wildlife. Look for nesting yellowhammers and whitethroats in the summer, feeding redwings and fieldfares in the winter, and small mammals such as bank voles and shrews at any time of year.

Some insects are particularly associated with hedges, such as the very rare black hairstreak butterfly which lives on blackthorn.

As well as their resident and visiting wildlife, hedges provide safe corridors for wildlife to travel between otherwise separate pieces of woodland – think of them as nature's cycle paths. You can sometimes see wild animals crossing at gateways, going from one hedge to the next.

Old and thick hedges provide food and shelter for a lot of wildlife.

Parks and gardens

Just because somewhere looks nice and tidy for people doesn't mean it won't work for wildlife. It's true that many parks and gardens aren't brilliant for wildflowers because any that appear get pulled out as weeds. But there is usually a forgotten corner with a few weeds growing through, or that hasn't had too many garden chemicals thrown on it. These are the places to look first for interesting minibeasts, which, in turn, provide food for other garden wildlife such as hedgehogs and robins.

However, a lot of garden wildlife simply goes unnoticed. Over 100 different types of moths visit most gardens every year, and garden soil can contain all sorts of goodies.

Also garden flowers can be full of nectar. Simpler, older varieties of flowers are often better than some of the more modern ones, and these will attract butterflies.

Tidy places

Many town or city parks look too tidy for much wildlife. Some will have old trees that have their own wildlife. Others may have ponds and lakes. However, whatever is there, some form of wildlife will usually move into it.

Country parks are often more interesting for wildlife.

Remember though, make sure that you have permission to look in any gardens and don't go wandering in areas of parkland on your own.

Even in the tidiest park, you'll find some wildlife.

Bees visit nectar-rich garden flowers.

Urban environments

Towns and cities can be great places for watching wildlife. In some places they are even better than the surrounding countryside because parks, gardens and waste ground provide a range of habitats that may no longer exist elsewhere in the area.

In general, if you are looking for wildlife in towns and cities, try to find the oldest, most run-down and wettest parts of town. Tidy modern places have less wildlife.

Almost every town river and canal will have its fish and water life. Park lakes and streams and rivers running through towns are great for birds, and will have plants that you won't find anywhere else.

On buildings

Some urban wildlife depends on buildings, from nesting swifts and house sparrows to roosting bats and garden hedgehogs. Old-fashioned sewage works, usually on the edge of town, provide some of the best places inland to see wading birds and the first swallows migrating through. Pied wagtails and starlings may roost in towns in winter because they will be warmer than the countryside.

Tall city buildings can provide nesting sites for birds of prey, including kestrels and peregrines, and old churchyards, especially the neglected corners, can have all sorts of wildflowers and insects. Don't forget to look at the lichens on the gravestones themselves – the dates will tell you how old the lichens could be.

Any cracks in pavements or walls will soon be colonised by wildflowers. Don't just think of them as weeds – they may have been around since before the city was built.

Keep your eyes open

The key for the urban wildlife watcher is just to keep your eyes open. You may spot gulls flying overhead on their way to roost for the night, ladybirds and zebra spiders on the walls and windowsills – and even moths and other insects splattered on the front number plates of cars in the supermarket car park!

House sparrows depend on buildings.

Most wildlife lives outdoors, but you will be able to find something alive in any home, however clean and tidy it is. There will be spiders, carpet mites and beetles, perhaps dog or cat fleas, the odd sleeping ladybird and lacewing, and maybe even mice. If your home isn't centrally heated, you may find silverfish, and perhaps even woodlice or slugs in damper patches. Occasionally a trail of ants may get in.

Your garage or shed is likely to have all these and more. If you leave windows open in the summer, all sorts of things may fly in!

Some wildlife, such as the daddy long-legs spider, is only ever found indoors in the UK! It usually lives in warmer climates farther south, but can survive here because we heat our homes to make them comfortable to live in.

If you get any new houseplants, you are likely to bring in more new animals. There may be tiny slugs that creep out of the soil. Very occasionally you may even find an exotic caterpillar in your shop-bought salad!

This daddy long-legs spider would not survive outside.

Wildlife everywhere

Wildlife really is everywhere. It's often a nuisance in the home – especially the beetle grubs or tiny moth caterpillars that eat natural fabrics or stored foods – but isn't it also amazing that such creatures choose to move in with us?

So before you decide to evict a newcomer from your home, take a good look at it, find out a bit more about it and enjoy it for its own sake. It's alive, it's here and it's fascinating!

Mammals

Did you know you're a mammal? Humans are mammals. We have things in common with all other mammals that help tell us apart from other creatures.

About mammals

- Mammals have hair. Fur is just a special sort of hair that traps more heat by having a thick under layer and then 'guard' hairs over it to keep warm air in.

- Mammals have moveable lips – this helps us to eat and talk, and sometimes, for other mammals, to investigate their world. Watch how a rabbit uses its lips to hold grass while it is chewing it.

- Mammals have live, wriggling babies. We don't lay eggs.

- Mammals feed their young milk that their mothers make. You very rarely see this in the wild because mothers like to keep their babies away from prying eyes and teeth.

- Mammals, like birds, regulate their body temperature. This means that most of us keep going, whatever the weather! The only mammals in the UK that hibernate are bats, hedgehogs and dormice.

The UK has about 46 species of land mammals, ranging from pygmy shrews that are about 8cm long to red deer that may be over 200cm long. We also have 18 species of bats, breeding Atlantic grey and common seals, and over 20 different whales and dolphins that visit our seas. If you see more than five species of mammals in a day you are doing well.

Hedgehogs are one of the UK's only hibernating mammals.

If you want to get a decent view of bigger mammals, such as otters, deer and foxes, you will need to creep up on them very slowly and carefully. Mostly, you will catch a glimpse through binoculars if you are lucky, or will be able to spot them from a hide.

Top tips for mammal watching

- Dawn and dusk are the best times to see most mammals.

- Wear dull, non-rustly clothes and a hat with a brim so that you break up your outline and don't scare the creatures.

- Stay downwind of mammals when you can. They have a much better sense of smell than we do. To most mammals, you are still smelly even when you're clean!

- If you see a mammal, stop still, don't stare straight at it and don't point at it or it will run away.

- Keep low and off the skyline, don't approach in a straight line and move slowly and quietly.

- Small mammals can be easier to see because they don't recognise people. Again, keep still and look through binoculars.

- If you see a mink, stoat or weasel, try making squeaking noises to attract it. They will often come quite close. Do the same to a rabbit and it will run away!

Squeaking noises encourage weasels to come closer.

Going batty!

Most of the sounds that bats make are too high for people to hear. This sound is called ultrasound. You may hear the odd high-pitched squeak, but even then you will be missing most of it. This is where bat detectors come in.

Sound is really important for bats. They find their way around and hunt flying insects, mainly moths, by shouting at them and listening for the echo that bounces back. Bats can tell whether there is a tree in front or a juicy moth – handy! Each different type of bat calls at a different pitch and in a different way.

Bat detectors

Bat detectors pick up this high-pitched sound and translate it into lower noises that we can hear and use to identify the bats. The cheapest bat detectors cost £30-40, but are well worth putting on your Christmas list. As well as bats, they are great for listening to crickets and grasshoppers. Jangle a bunch of keys in front of a bat detector and be amazed at how much ultrasound they pick up.

A brown long-eared bat has big ears to catch sounds.

Bats

Our 18 bat species are our only flying mammals. They all hibernate in the winter when there are no flying insects for them to eat.

Brown long-eared bat (25cm wingspan)

Identification: Looks about the size of a starling in flight. Huge ears, nearly as long as its body, and big eyes (for a bat).

Behaviour: Flies quite slowly about 6m above the ground. Picks insects from tree leaves as well as catching them in flight.

Fact: Long-eared are much quieter than other bats so are hard to find with a bat detector.

Where to see it: Parks, gardens and woodland edges. Roosts in groups of up to 30 in trees or older buildings.

Don't confuse with: Other bats. But if you can see the ears, this bat is obvious.

Daubenton's bat (25cm wingspan)

Identification: Often called the water bat because it is usually seen low over calm, clear water – the smoother the better.

Behaviour: Catches insects hatching from still water – ponds, canals, and slow-moving rivers.

Fact: This bat was named in honour of an 18th Century French naturalist.

Where to see it: Look for open water near trees. They come out around an hour after sunset on summer nights.

Don't confuse with: Other bats, which look similar in flight. This is the main one that patrols over water.

Insect eaters

Worms and insects can feed much bigger animals, such as these.

Pygmy shrew (8.5mm, including tail)

Identification: A tiny, hyperactive grey-brown mammal with a long, flexible snout and short thick tail.

Behaviour: Munches its way through more than its own body weight of insects, spiders and woodlice every day.

Fact: This is our smallest mammal, but has one of our largest fleas living on it – it's bigger than the shrew's eye!

Where to see it: Pygmy shrews live all over the UK in long grass and wooded areas.

Don't confuse with: Common and water shrews, which are both larger. No other small mammals have such snuffly looking noses.

Hedgehog (Up to 30cm long)

Identification: Our only spiky mammal. Brown and round, but with surprisingly long legs when running.

Behaviour: Usually on short grass, in woodlands or on lawns, where it hunts for slugs, snails and earthworms to eat. Makes loud grunts and squeals in early summer.

Fact: Although hedgehogs famously hibernate, they may wake up several times in a winter and move house.

Where to see it: Suburban gardens, and woodland edges throughout the UK, except on a few remote islands.

Don't confuse with: Hedgehogs are unmistakable!

Rabbit and hares

Together, these long-legged jumpers are called lagomorphs. We have three species in the UK.

Rabbit (40cm)

Identification: Grey-brown and very rounded, with long back legs, long ears and big, alert eyes on the side of their head. A short white tail sticks up as they bound away.

Behaviour: Usually keeps within a few hundred metres of its burrow. Eats grass and crops. Left undisturbed, can sometimes be seen sunbathing, but usually comes out at dusk. Live in communities called warrens.

Fact: Generally silent, but squeals in distress. Males may thump the ground with their back legs to warn of approaching danger.

Where to see it: Almost anywhere that they can dig and find food, including sand dunes, woodland edges, hedgerows, large gardens and roadsides.

Don't confuse with: Hares, which are larger, have even longer back legs and black-tipped ears and black on the tail.

Brown hare (50-60cm)

Identification: More red brown than mountain hare (which turns white in winter), and much bigger and more angular than rabbits. Staring yellow eyes if you can get close enough to see.

Behaviour: Females can be seen fighting males off in the spring mating season, but often you will just see them sitting in fields. They are most active at night and are usually alone.

Fact: Brown hares can run at speeds of up to 45 mph. Brown hares spend the day in a slight dip in the ground called a form.

Where to see it: Wide open country, especially farmland.

Don't confuse with: Mountain hare, which is more rabbit-like and turns white in winter. It is also blue-grey in summer, except in Ireland, where it is brown!

Small rodents

Scurrying little vegetarians. Most don't live longer than a year.

Field vole (110mm long)

Identification: Small grey-brown and short tailed and round. Smaller eyes and shorter, blunter face than rats, mice or shrews.

Behaviour: Forms little tracks and runs in old damp grassland, where it spends most of its time eating grass.

Fact: There are more field voles in the UK than there are people.

Where to see it: Even though they are so common, your best chance of seeing a vole is either its remains in an owl pellet or by trapping, perhaps at a river bank.

Don't confuse with: Bank vole, which is redder and has a longer tail. Water vole is much larger and is usually seen swimming away.

Harvest mouse (50-70mm long)

Identification: Our smallest mouse has a tail that it can use as a gripping and climbing tool. It has hairy ears and a gingery colour.

Behaviour: Clambers through reeds and corn using its tail as an extra limb. Weaves a tennis-ball sized nest close to ground level.

Fact: Declined massively with changes in farming, so is now more common in reedbeds than in corn fields.

Where to see it: Mainly in England, from Yorkshire southwards. Look around the edges of cornfields and reedbeds for nests. The animals themselves stay well hidden.

Don't confuse with: Wood mouse. Its hairy ears and useful tail tell this apart.

Red squirrel and mole

Up in the trees or burrowing underground – these are perfectly adapted to their homes.

Red squirrel (35cm long including tail)

Identification: Red to grey brown on top and pale underneath with tufted ears (especially in winter) and a bushy red tail.

Behaviour: Mainly scampering around in pinewoods, but will also come to the ground and feed on peanuts in bird feeders. Active for most of the year.

Fact: Red squirrels are much rarer in Britain than they used to be, but are still the main squirrel in Ireland and most of mainland Europe.

Where to see it: Now mainly in Scotland and Ireland, but also in a few places in northern England and Wales, plus outposts on the Isle of Wight, and Brownsea Island in Dorset.

Don't confuse with: The much larger grey squirrel, which can look a bit brownish, but never so red as these.

Mole (12cm long)

Identification: Very short, black or grey fur, paddle-like feet, small eyes and a long snout. Surprisingly quick movements above ground.

Behaviour: Spends almost its whole life underground in tunnels, coming up only to avoid flooding or for young ones to find a new place to live.

Fact: Super-sized mole hills, called fortresses, may contain several nests and are often built on slightly higher ground to avoid flooding.

Where to see it: You can see evidence of moles in most habitats – mole hills and tunnels just breaking the surface sometimes, but not in Ireland. Seeing a live mole is quite rare.

Don't confuse with: Unmistakeable!

Carnivores

Fish and meat eaters have forward-facing eyes and sharp teeth for hunting.

Otter (up to 130cm long)

Identification: Bigger than many people think. Dark brown, sleek and streamlined. Short legs and a strong-looking tail. Noticeable hump at the hip.

Behaviour: Classic fish-eater, always in or near water. Often nocturnal on English rivers, but sometimes comes out during the day, especially on Scottish islands.

Voice: High-pitched squeaking sounds keep the family in contact, but often completely silent.

Where to see it: Now recorded in every county, but elusive.

Don't confuse with: The much bolder mink, which is much smaller and has longer darker fur.

Fox (105cm long including 40cm tail)

Identification: Dog-like but with a lighter build and bushier tail. Orange-red fur above and white below. Tail has a white tip.

Behaviour: Hunters and scavengers, foxes will eat anything and live anywhere. They raise their cubs in a simple dug-out den, called an earth.

Voice: A barking yelp and various shrieks tell you that foxes are around.

Where to see it: Although there are far more foxes in the countryside than in towns and cities, the urban ones are often easier to see because they are less scared of people.

Don't confuse with: Medium-sized dogs, which can look similar, but are rarely as slender.

Badger (90cm long)

Identification: Stocky, short-legged. Grey above and black below with distinctive black-and-white head stripes.

Behaviour: Families live together and come out from their burrows, called a sett, at night to hunt worms and fruits.

Fact: There are about 200,000 badgers in the UK, but most people have never seen a live one.

Where to see it: Best seen by waiting quietly downwind of an active sett at dusk. Badgers live throughout the UK, especially where the ground is dry enough to dig burrows without their flooding.

Don't confuse with: Unmistakeable!

Polecat (50cm long including tail)

Identification: Short-legged and long tailed. These agile creatures have black-and tan fur and a dark bandit mask over a pale face.

Behaviour: Polecats are slim enough to hunt rabbits in their burrows, but they tend to hunt rats in the winter.

Fact: The polecat is the ancestor of the domestic ferret.

Where to see it: Polecats are spreading back through Britain (but they never lived in Ireland) and are usually shy. One or two people have set up watching schemes, but otherwise you will just have to be really lucky.

Don't confuse with: Domestic ferrets, which are the same species and may even be the same colour.

Wildcat (about 80cm including tail)

Identification: Like a large, stripy tabby cat, with a thick, blunt-tipped tail. Never tame enough to come for a stroke!

Behaviour: Very shy and generally nocturnal. These hunters rely on catching small mammals.

Fact: Wildcats used to live throughout Britain and Ireland but people either hunted them or removed their habitat.

Where to see it: These are really hard to spot, even in the Scottish Highlands where they live. You may see one in a zoo, but to find one in the wild is a once-in-a-lifetime treat.

Don't confuse with: Big domestic cats, which can look similar, but rarely so fierce.

For such fierce hunters, wildcats are very shy of people.

Seals

Sleek and streamlined for swimming and hunting fish – but faster on land than you might think.

Grey seal (up to 200cm long)

Identification: The larger of our two seals. Usually grey or brown and often spotty, but darker when wet. Looks down its arched Roman nose and opens and shuts its vertical nostrils.

Behaviour: Grey seals come ashore to breed in the autumn but spend most of their time at sea hunting fish.

Voice: Various snorts, grunts and long strained whistling calls can sound quite human from a distance.

Where to see it: Over half the world's grey seals live around our coasts, so they can pop up anywhere, but they have traditional pupping grounds, such as the Farne Islands and Blakeney Point that can best be visited on boat trips.

Don't confuse with: Common seal, which is smaller with a more dog-like face. If you see something at sea with a fin on its back, it's a fish, whale or dolphin.

Common seal (up to 150cm long)

Identification: The smaller of our two seals, with a dog-like face, long whiskers and finer spots. Its nostrils line up like the letter V.

Behaviour: Spends most of its time at sea, but comes ashore to have its pup and to moult its fur in the summer.

Voice: Sad singing that used to be thought of as mermaids.

Where to see it: Common seal is rarer in Britain than grey seal, but more common in Ireland. They visit traditional sites each year, sometimes with greys. Often seen off the coast, especially in Scotland.

Don't confuse with: Grey seals, which are bigger, blotchier and have vertical nostrils.

Whales and dolphins

Despite living at sea, these all have to come to the surface to breathe air – and sometimes we can see them.

Bottle-nosed dolphin (up to 4m long)

Identification: Dark grey, with a clear, but short 'beak' (really its mouth) and a tall fin on the centre of its back.

Behaviour: Usually in groups and generally seen jumping clear from the water. Dolphins spend their time hunting fish in groups.

Voice: Various high-pitched squeaks and whistles that we don't understand.

Where to see it: Your best bet is to either look from a high headland on a calm day or from a ferry. In a few places, such as the Moray Firth, groups of dolphins regularly come close to land.

Don't confuse with: Other dolphins. But this is the commonest of five species of dolphin that occur in UK waters.

Harbour porpoise (up to 1.8m long)

Identification: Dark with a short, blunt head. The fin on its back is quite short.

Behaviour: Usually breaks the water surface only to breathe, so rarely breaches. Hunts alone or in groups of up to five individuals, often near the shore.

Voice: As the name suggests, porpoises sometimes come into harbours or even up rivers.

Where to see it: You could be lucky from any of our coasts, but they are rarest in the Channel. They are most commonly seen in spring and summer.

Don't confuse with: Other dolphins and pilot whales. Look for the rounded head and small size.

Killer whale or Orca (around 7m long)

Identification: Black above and white below with a tall triangular dorsal fin and white patch above and behind the eye.

Behaviour: Social and intelligent killer of fish, birds and other sea mammals – but not humans so it is still safe to go into the water!

Voice: Very complex range of squeaks, clicks and whistles used to keep in touch with the rest of the family and to coordinate hunting.

Where to see it: Killer whales come to the waters of north and east Scotland regularly, but not predictably enough to plan a holiday around.

Don't confuse with: Unmistakeable if seen clearly, but pilot whale is a similar shape.

Minke whale (up to 9m long)

Identification: Quite small (for a whale!) and with a pointed snout. Dark back and pale belly, always with a white mark on its flippers.

Behaviour: Usually on its own, this whale visits our seas in search of a wide range of fish and crustaceans.

Voice: As loud as a jet aeroplane taking off, and similarly mechanical.

Where to see it: Whale watching trips from the Isle of Man and west Scotland are your best bet, along with longer ferry journeys. They rarely visit southern or eastern coasts.

Don't confuse with: Other similar whales, which are much larger. Pilot whales have a much more rounded head.

Deer

Nimble and built for running and jumping – to escape the wolves we no longer have.

Muntjac (1m long)

Identification: Our smallest deer. About the size of a Labrador dog, but darker, rounder, with spindly legs and very short tails. Short antlers and black stripes on the face.

Behaviour: Visits woodland and gardens where it can be quite bold and can wreak havoc with wildflowers.

Voice: A harsh, repeated bark, rather like a dog's, usually given at dusk or at night.

Where to see it: Along the edges of woodlands (and sometimes major roads) and in larger parks, gardens and churchyards.

Don't confuse with: A running dog or Chinese water deer, which are rarer and more ginger in colour than dark brown.

Red deer (up to 2.3m long)

Identification: Our biggest deer. Males, called stags, have huge spiky antlers. The females, called hinds, don't. Both are mainly a rich red-brown colour.

Behaviour: Usually in single-sex herds for most of the year, but males come together to fight for females in the autumn mating season, called the rut.

Voice: Rutting stags make loud bellowing calls.

Where to see it: Across moors and hills, especially across Scotland and south-west England, but also in deer parks in other places.

Don't confuse with: Sika deer, which look very similar and may interbreed with red deer. Fallow deer usually look spotty and have flatter antlers.

Birds

You know what birds are, but have you thought about what makes them different from other animals? They are the only living creatures with feathers.

About birds

All our birds are adapted for flight. Their main bones are lightweight and hollow, their chest muscles are huge so they can cope with flapping wings and they have light beaks with no teeth rather than heavy jaws.

You can see birds in any habitat at any time of day or year. There are around 300 different birds that you could expect to see in the UK regularly, with another 200 or so more that turn up only rarely.

Many people get especially excited by the chance of seeing these rarities and will go out of their way to see rare birds that other people have spotted. This is called twitching. Other people just seek out the best birds they can wherever they go, or even just in gardens or school grounds. You can take an interest in birds as far as you want.

You can see kestrels hovering in search of food throughout the UK.

Watching birds

Even on a poor day's birdwatching you are likely to see more and be able to identify more of what you see than with any other group of wild animals. No wonder birdwatching is the most popular form of watching wildlife. Even if you aren't interested in numbers, the variety, visibility and things that birds do make them an ideal introduction to the world of wildlife.

Birdwatching is possible with no special kit, but binoculars will make your life much easier and more fun. A telescope and tripod can be good, too, but they are expensive and awkward.

Top birdwatching tips

- Look everywhere for birds and at any time of year or day.

- Always take binoculars with you.

- Have a notebook and pencil with you.

- If you have a smartphone, get a bird identification app for the sounds.

- Listen well. Experienced bird 'watchers' are bird listeners first.

- Carry a field guide in your bag.

- Go where other birdwatchers go – people know the best places to see birds more than other wildlife.

- Look up which birds live in new places and habitats before you visit.

- Enjoy looking at birds – it doesn't have to be hard work.

The goldfinch is becoming more common – find one near you.

Feathers

When identifying birds, it is helpful to know what the main feathers are called. Describe the colours and patterns on those and you are a long way towards identifying the birds. Luckily for us, all birds have the same types of feathers:

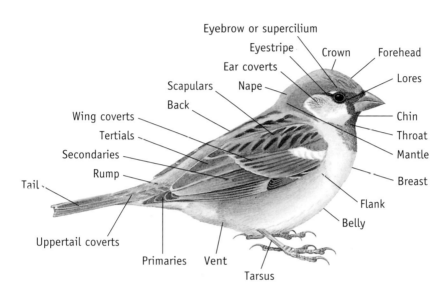

Eyebrow or supercilium
Eyestripe
Ear coverts
Crown
Forehead
Lores
Scapulars
Nape
Back
Wing coverts
Chin
Tertials
Throat
Secondaries
Mantle
Rump
Breast
Tail
Flank
Uppertail coverts
Belly
Primaries
Vent
Tarsus

You can see and hear magpies in both town and country.

83

Wildfowl

Ducks, geese and swans are together known as wildfowl. Millions of them visit the UK every winter.

Wigeon (42-52cm long)

Identification: Round-headed, gentle-looking duck more often seen in pairs or large flocks than on its own. The male has a chestnut head, grey body and black tail. The female is much browner.

Behaviour: Wigeons come out of the water to graze, but they never go far from the safety of open water. They also spend time dabbling in shallow water and mud. In late winter, before most of them return to Siberia to breed, wigeons pair up. This is an ideal time to get familiar with female ducks that generally don't have such bright markings as the males.

Voice: A far-carrying whistling call that rises quickly and falls more slowly.

Where to see it: In winter around a million wigeons arrive here, so you will see them on most larger lakes, reservoirs and estuaries.

Don't confuse with: The smaller teal or bigger mallard. Unlike the diving ducks, their tails tend to stick out of the water.

Barnacle goose (55-70cm long)

Identification: A compact, black-and-white goose with a black neck and a white face.

Behaviour: Barnacle geese fly in classic V formations, and graze on grass on Scottish islands.

Voice: Yaps like a small dog.

Where to see it: Winter visitor from Greenland in large numbers to north and west Scotland and Ireland, but some released birds also breed in southern England.

Don't confuse with: Brent goose, which has a black face, or Canada goose, which is much larger, and has a brown back.

Wading birds

Birds in various families, but all with long legs for walking in water.

Little egret (60cm long)

Identification: Small, pure white heron with a black beak, black legs and yellow feet. Breeding pairs have long, flowing white plume feathers growing from the back of their heads, and finer plumes on their back and breast.

Behaviour: Stalks fish along the edges of saltmarsh pools, but also roosts in trees, sometimes in large flocks.

Voice: Occasional croaks, but usually silent.

Where to see it: Now seen throughout the UK, having first bred in southern England in 1998. Look for it on saltmarshes and wetland nature reserves, but don't be surprised if one turns up at your local park lake.

Don't confuse with: Great white egret, which is much bigger and has a yellow beak. Cattle egret is stockier and has a stubbier yellow beak.

Moorhen (35cm long)

Identification: Can look black at a distance, but their head, neck and undersides are dark blue and the back is greeny-brown. Long green legs with red 'knees' and very long toes. White stripe along the side and a constantly flicked tail with white underneath. Yellow-tipped red beak and red forehead.

Behaviour: Either swimming on the water with flicky tail, or walking on grass where their fantastic feet become more obvious. Often in loose flocks.

Voice: A harsh, explosive 'Krruruck' or various 'ke ke ke ke ke' calls. Moorhens are quite vocal.

Where to see it: Almost any river, lake or large pond will have moorhens. They are found in even smaller wet places than coots.

Don't confuse with: Coots, which are bigger, and blacker all over with a bold white forehead and beak, and no white on the tail or sides.

Waders

Long-legged lovers of watery places – expect to see waders mainly at the coast.

Curlew (55cm long)

Identification: Our largest wader. It is mainly brown, but has a very long and distinctly down-curved beak and long legs that may look grey or blue.

Behaviour: Digs its beak deep into estuary mud in search of worms and crabs, but also walks along, picking small creatures from under stones. In the summer, it nests on moorlands where it feeds along river banks.

Voice: Lovely 'cour-lwee, cour-lwee' often given in flight.

Where to see it: Anywhere around the coast, on estuaries, mudflats and saltmarshes or in wetland reserves throughout the year. On high moorland in the summer.

Don't confuse with: The smaller and rarer whimbrel, which has a shorter beak and stripy head.

Lapwing (30cm long)

Identification: Can look black-and-white from a distance, but is really a shimmering green on top, with a black chest and white underneath. It has a long crest and pink legs.

Behaviour: Stop-go-stop-go feeding motion is typical of the plovers. Often seen flying in flocks that seem to blink black-and-white against the sky.

Where to see it: It nests in farmland and often winters in flocks on ploughed fields, but you will see more of them on estuaries all around the UK.

Don't confuse with: Oystercatcher, which is more black and white, with a long red beak and no crest.

Birds of prey and owls

Sharp, forward-facing eyes and hooked beaks, but no wiser than other birds.

Barn owl (35cm long)

Identification: May look completely white, especially in car headlights at night, but its upperside is a soft fawn/tan colour. Broad stiff wings and low flight over the same patch of ground again and again.

Behaviour: May perch for hours on a fence post, but usually seen flying quite low over rough fields, concentrating on the ground.

Voice: Completely silent when hunting, but makes blood-curdling shrieks in search of a mate. Chicks make all sorts of squeaks and hisses when disturbed.

Where to see it: Across pasture land, saltmarshes and wetlands across the UK. Often nests in old farm buildings and can sometimes be seen in daylight.

Don't confuse with: Short-eared and long-eared owls, which are darker with longer wings.

Sparrowhawk (33-40cm long)

Identification: Rounded wings, long tail and vivid yellow eye, and barred underneath. Adult males are grey on top, youngsters and females are dark brown.

Behaviour: Often seen flying with distinctive flap-flap-glide wing action, or zipping over a garden hedge at top speed to surprise a finch.

Where to see it: In woodlands and gardens across the UK, but rarer in the uplands.

Don't confuse with: Kestrels, which usually have pointier wings and hover. They also rarely visit town gardens.

Seabirds

The UK has a special duty to look after these mostly black and white fish eaters – because we have more than almost anyone else.

Gannet (94cm long but 172cm wing span)

Identification: Adults are huge and sparkling white with black wing tips, a dagger-like beak and yellow heads. Youngsters are dark brown, but you may see in-betweenies.

Behaviour: Skims the waves until it finds a shoal of fish then catches them by plunging into the sea from a great height.

Voice: Silent at sea, but lots of deep croaking sounds at nest colonies.

Where to see it: From any headland, especially in spring and autumn, but best at one of their nesting sites, such as Bempton Cliffs in Yorkshire or Bass Rock in East Lothian.

Don't confuse with: Gulls, but gannet is much bigger and longer-winged. More like a small albatross!

Guillemot (40cm long)

Identification: Dark chocolate brown above and white beneath, but very like a small flying penguin.

Behaviour: Nests on cliffs, but spends all the rest of its time at sea, where it dives deeper than any other British bird after sand eels.

Voice: Whinnying 'aaaaaarrr' call at the nest colonies.

Where to see it: At nesting cliffs from March to July. After that, you may be lucky enough to see one off any bit of coast, but hardly ever inland.

Don't confuse with: Puffin, which is smaller with the famous coloured beak, or razorbill, which is blacker with a much thicker beak.

Farmland birds

Farmland birds often find the ways we grow food just right for them, especially the older ways.

Yellowhammer (16cm long)

Identification: Dumpy little yellow bird with a chestnut rump and variable amount of brown streaking on the body. Females are browner.

Behaviour: Found feeding in arable fields and hedgerows, and in mixed flocks with other buntings and finches in winter. Sings later into the summer than most birds.

Voice: Famously, its song sounds like 'a little bit of bread and no cheese' but it often forgets to mention the cheese.

Where to see it: More common on English farmland than in other UK countries, but still widespread throughout the UK.

Don't confuse with: Great tit, which has a green back or yellow wagtail, which is much slimmer. But few other birds are as yellow.

Grey partridge (30cm long)

Identification: Very rounded, with a grey body, chestnut face and rusty horseshoe mark on its belly.

Behaviour: Creeps around in little groups in arable fields, saltmarshes and even sand dunes.

Voice: Harsh, repetitive, mechanical 'kee-chick'.

Where to see it: Much rarer than it used to be, but look in open fields or wait as they fly back on to farmland as the tide rises on a saltmarsh. Very rare in west Scotland and Northern Ireland.

Don't confuse with: Red-legged partridge, which has white face and black eyestripe.

Woodland birds

You can find birds anywhere in woods, from the tips of thin twigs to the woodland floor.

Goldcrest (9cm long – tiny!)

Identification: Along with the rare firecrest, this is our smallest bird. Pale green above, with a beady eye, sad moustache and yellow crown stripe. Murky white below.

Behaviour: Delicately picks its way through pine trees, either on its own or in small flocks, especially in winter.

Voice: Very high-pitched 'see' call that many adults can't hear at all.

Where to see it: Mixed woodland and hedgerows and the edges of conifer plantations. Sometimes in gardens, but rarely visits feeders.

Don't confuse with: Firecrest, which has a stripier head – and is much rarer. Wren, which is brown, not green.

Coal tit (12cm long)

Identification: The least colourful of our tits, with a white patch on the back of its black head.

Behaviour: At home in pinewoods, but also visits gardens, where it nips in to grab a sunflower seed from a feeder before flying away to eat it or store it for the winter.

Voice: High-pitched 'one-two one-two' song.

Where to see it: Keep a look out at your bird table, or in winter flocks with other tits, but any woodland will have coal tits.

Don't confuse with: Blue and great tits are much more colourful and a little bigger. The rarer marsh and willow tits are both browner but lack the white patch on the back of the head.

Song thrush (23cm long)

Identification: A little smaller and shorter tailed than a blackbird, with a warm brown back and heart-shaped spots underneath on a pale cream body.

Behaviour: Feeds mainly on the ground, where it catches snails and bashes the shells off them on a stone.

Voice: Beautiful loud, clear song made up of repeated phrases.

Where to see it: If you are lucky, you may see one on your garden lawn. If not, look along old hedges and woodland rides.

Don't confuse with: The larger mistle thrush is greyer and has bolder, less tidy black blotchy spots underneath. Female blackbird is brown all over rather than having a pale but spotty underside.

Jackdaw (34cm long)

Identification: Small, tidy swaggering crow, with a pale eye. Black all over except for grey back of the neck.

Behaviour: Often on rooftops where it may nest in chimneys, but it prefers a hole in a tree. Often joins other crows and rooks in flocks in fields.

Voice: Cackling 'jack' or 'chack'.

Where to see it: common in towns and cities as well as on sea cliffs and in woodlands. Rare in upland Britain.

Don't confuse with: Carrion crow, rook and raven, which are all larger with pure black feathers all over. Hooded crow, which has a grey body rather than just a grey neck.

Reptiles and amphibians

These two groups are often talked about together, even though they are quite different. Our land reptiles are either snakes or lizards. There are also half a dozen sea turtles that visit occasionally, with leatherback being the most common. Our amphibians are frogs, toads or newts.

Snakes

We have only three native species of snake, the grass snake, the very rare smooth snake and the adder (or viper). The adder is our only venomous snake, but it very rarely bites people. It is much more likely to slither away or to hiss a warning if it is cornered.

Lizards

We have two native legged lizards, the common and sand lizards, plus the slow-worm. Slow-worms aren't worms and they aren't slow! They are legless lizards, which makes them look rather like snakes. They do, however have eyelids (snakes don't), and can drop their tail if they need to escape, just like their leggy relatives.

Amphibians

Reptiles have dry, scaly skin, but amphibians keep their skin damp and have to return to water to breed, even if they spend much of their time on land. Our amphibians with tails are the three newts, smooth or common newt, palmate newt, and great crested newt. They look like damp, slow-moving lizards. They are usually seen in ponds, but may spend the winter tucked under bark or in a wood pile.

Common frog and common toad are our most common tailless amphibians – but even they have tails as tadpoles. There is also the very rare natterjack toad that lives on coastal sand dune ponds.

Common lizards can sometimes be found warming up at the start of the day.

Look for newts in ponds in summer.

Cold-blooded creatures

If you were to take a frog's temperature on a cold day, it would be lower than on a hot day. However, yours wouldn't be, unless you were ill. This is why we call reptiles and amphibians cold-blooded. It just means they use the Sun's warmth to get them up to operating temperatures.

Morning watch

This is useful for us warm-blooded nature watchers because we can be up and active and looking for snakes before they have warmed up enough to slide away. Find a large, open, sheltered south-facing surface, such as a big stone or a log. Watch it carefully early on spring and summer mornings and you may be lucky enough to spot a reptile. Later in the day, it would hear you coming and have the energy to run away.

First thing in the morning, you may find a slow-worm or lizard warming up under a sheet of corrugated iron in long grass. If you can get hold of some black roofing felt, why not put some of that down in a hot spot in your garden and look under it in the morning?

A common toad uses the Sun's warmth to keep moving.

Water watching

Amphibians are also cold-blooded, so look for them in the warm shallows of lakes and ponds. Raising tadpoles from frogspawn is easy and fun and you should be able to get many through to tiny frog stage. Remember to release them back into the pond you caught them in to avoid spreading disease between ponds.

Newts are easily caught in pond nets and can be given a thorough examination in a dipping tray. Then let them go again unharmed.

Snakes and lizards

Smooth skinned and fast, these predators only come out in the summer.

Adder (up to 90cm long)

Identification: Quite a fat snake with bold zigzag marking all down the back. Can vary from almost black to very pale brown. No bright yellow collar.

Behaviour: Usually seen warming itself up in the mornings in a favoured sunny spot. Hunts small mammals and lizards.

Fact: This is our only venomous snake but it very rarely bites people. It prefers to escape. The bite is painful and serious but hardly ever kills people.

Where to see it: On heathland and grasslands throughout Britain, but sadly not in Ireland.

Don't confuse with: Grass snake, which is green with a yellow neck collar and usually seen in water. Smooth snake is very rare, is slimmer and usually has a line of spots down its back.

Common lizard (up to 15cm long)

Identification: Quite plain looking, usually brown, but sometimes grey or pale green. Thin stripes run down the sides of its body.

Behaviour: Runs very fast to catch insects to eat, but spends a lot of time watching and waiting, especially on old wood.

Fact: The lizard lives all the way north into the Arctic Circle.

Where to see it: Heathlands and old grasslands throughout the UK.

Don't confuse with: Sand lizard, which is much bigger and more colourful. Newts look damp and are very slow on land.

Amphibians

These creatures like to stay damp. They breathe through their skin as well as with their lungs.

Common frog (up to 9cm body length)

Identification: Mostly green or brown, with blotching, including a dark patch behind the eye. The back has a definite hump.

Behaviour: Frogs spend more time in wet grass than in ponds, but are expert swimmers, jumpers and fly catchers.

Fact: Mostly silent, but spring evening churring calls suggest that males are looking to mate. Only American frogs go 'ribbit'!

Where to see it: Garden ponds, lakes and wet moorlands throughout the UK. Frogs will lay their eggs, called spawn, in almost any puddle.

Don't confuse with: Toads, which have drier, lumpier skin, are generally plainer brown and lack the eye patch.

Great crested newt (up to 16cm long)

Identification: A big warty newt. Black or nearly so above and with orange spots underneath. Males are bigger and darker than females and have a spiky crest in the summer.

Behaviour: Outside the summer breeding season, newts are found under logs or in other damp places, but up to a mile from their ponds.

Fact: Each male crested newt has a unique pattern of spots on its tummy.

Where to see it: This is rare but found in some ponds almost all over England. It is rarer in Scotland and Wales and absent from Ireland.

Don't confuse with: Other newts, which are paler and smaller. Lizards are scaly and fast-moving.

Fish

All fish spend their entire lives in water, except for the odd leap here and there. They lay eggs and breathe through gills, and generally have streamlined bodies so that they can swim easily. Beyond that, there is huge variation. Fish are every bit as interesting as many other groups.

About fish

The most primitive fish are the sharks, skates and rays that live in the sea. Dogfish and porbeagle are our most common sharks, but they are tiny. We also have basking sharks up the west coast of Britain every summer. These are huge and harmless. Isn't it brilliant that the second biggest fish in the whole of the sea can be seen from our western cliff tops?

Flatfish are important for food for people, and our estuaries are flatfish breeding grounds. They are brilliant creatures. Many people will be familiar with them from big aquariums, but you can sometimes find baby flatfish in rockpools, or see them skitter away as you paddle slowly through the shallow water on a sandy beach.

Eels and salmon are two species that spend some of their time at sea and the rest – during their breeding season – in rivers. We also have many much smaller fish in our lakes, rivers and canals. However, a lot of anglers have released fish in these places for sport so their distribution is often not natural.

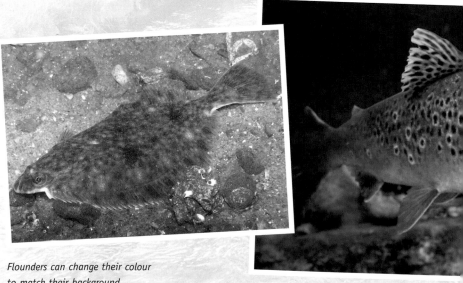

Flounders can change their colour to match their background.

Catching fish is more popular than watching them, but fish are fine creatures in their own right, if difficult to observe in the wild.

The easiest fish to spot while staying dry will usually be in clear shallow rivers or canals. You can sometimes see trout, pike, perch or even bream from a bridge.

Fish spotting tips

- Choose a bright day so that light penetrates the water.

- You may need to keep low down so that the fish doesn't spot you against the sky.

- Wear sunglasses with polarising lenses to cut through reflections on the water.

- Look for the smoothest water you can and a pale riverbed.

- If you catch minnows or sticklebacks – tiddlers – make sure to let them go where you found them when you have had a good look.

- Explore fish in seaside rockpools – you may find gobies, blennies and butterfish, baby flatfish and others trapped by the rising tide.

- In the sea, swim with a snorkel and mask over seaweed on an incoming tide and you may see wrasse, sea-pout and sand-eels. Don't do this alone, though. Also, remember only to do this on beaches where you know it is safe to swim.

Use a snorkel and mask to get a closer look at sea wildlife.

Some brown trouts spend time at sea, but they all breed in fresh water.

Freshwater fish

Always expect river fish to be facing upstream – they are streamlined to point into the current.

Pike (up to 1.5m long)

Identification: The streamlined shape, with a dorsal fin near to the tail and a huge toothy alligator grin, is distinctive, but expect the colours and patterns to vary.

Behaviour: Pike are fierce predators that spend a lot of time in the shallows of lakes and rivers, gradually creeping up on other fish before darting after them with lightning speed – exciting fish!

Fact: Pike can live for up to 30 years.

Where to see it: Lakes, reservoirs and slow-moving streams all over the UK. Look from bridges for the spear shape hanging still in the water.

Don't confuse with: The pike's body shape and patient watching are distinctive. Trout may look similar from above, but they are always moving.

Three-spined stickleback (8cm long)

Identification: These small fish have three spines sticking out of their back. Breeding males have red tummies and blue eyes.

Behaviour: Male sticklebacks defend a breeding territory, and invite females in to lay their eggs. It is the male who looks after the eggs.

Fact: The redder the male, the more successful he is likely to be.

Where to see it: Slow-moving streams and larger ponds, but also found in the sea.

Don't confuse with: 10-spined stickleback, which looks longer. Minnows lack the spines.

Seafish

Wildlife exists everywhere – even in your local chip shop!

Atlantic mackerel (20-50cm)

Identification: Silver-white below with blue-green stripes above. This animal is built for speed. Its fins even fold into streamlined slots when it wants to escape quickly.

Behaviour: Mackerel hunt together in huge schools that come close to land every summer to catch smaller fish and prawns.

Fact: Each female mackerel can lay over half a million eggs in a year.

Where to see it: These beautiful fish live all around our shores, which is why mackerel fishing trips are so common. You can often see dead ones in a fishmonger's display.

Don't confuse with: This is one of 10 species in the family that have been caught in British waters. Others include the famous blue-fin and skipjack tunas.

Basking shark (up to about 12m long)

Identification: A huge, harmless, dark grey shark, with a massive mouth that it holds open almost all the time. From land, you need to be sure that you can see both a dorsal fin (on its back) and the tail fin poking out of the water as the shark feeds on tiny creatures near the surface.

Behaviour: Basking sharks follow their food by migrating up the south and west coasts of Britain and Ireland in the summer before heading back out into the Atlantic for the rest of the year.

Fact: This is the second biggest fish in the sea (only the whale shark is bigger), but it eats some of the smallest creatures – just lots of them!

Where to see it: Cornish, Irish and Scottish headland. A few tourist boats search for them, but even they don't always find them.

Don't confuse with: Whales and dolphins, which only have one fin breaking the water surface.

Insects

Insects are all around us all the time, from the fleas on your dog to the moths at your windows on a summer evening. Insects are the most diverse group of creatures on the planet, but they all have a few things in common.

About insects

Insects have a clear three-part body plan: head, thorax and abdomen. The head is the sensory hub, where the eyes and the mouth are, the thorax is the segment where an insect's six legs, and also the wings that most of them have, grow from, and the abdomen is where digestion and reproduction occur. This body plan is probably easiest to see in ants, wasps and bees, but it is the same in other insects.

The study of insects is called entomology. There are still things about insects that are unknown to science that you can help discover. For example, we don't know what every UK caterpillar eats in the wild.

Insects have some of the most amazing lifestyles. There is the change from egg to caterpillar to chrysalis and flying adult that all our butterflies and moths go through. And what about the mayflies that live underwater as larvae for a year and then hatch, fly and mate in just a few hours before dying?

All insects have six legs and a head-thorax-abdomen body plan.

Insects take some outwitting! Three ways that insect watchers often use to find out which insects live in a place are with pooters, pitfall traps and tree-beating.

Pooter

A pooter is a handy device for capturing small insects unharmed and containing them while you have a good look. You can make one yourself easily, following this diagram:

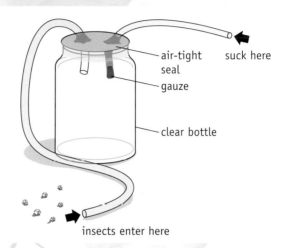

air-tight seal

suck here

gauze

clear bottle

insects enter here

Use it to suck up insects and spiders that are smaller than the entrance to the tube. Place your tube near the insect and take a sharp breath on the other tube. Don't blow – you will steam up the pot! Try to collect several similar insects together unless you want your pooter to become a battlefield of predator and prey.

Pitfall traps

Sink empty yoghurt pots into soil or a lawn right up to the brim. Leave them overnight and check in the morning to see what has fallen in. It's best to do this when you know there won't be any rain overnight. You can't be sure of catching swimmers!

Tree-beating

Lay an old sheet or open a large umbrella under a low branch and then knock the branch sharply. You'll take various minibeasts by surprise and they will drop off on to your sheet, where you can inspect them. Catch them with your pooter if you like.

Containers

You can buy tubes for holding insects, but the best thing is a bug-box. This has a magnifying glass built into the lid so that you can get a good look at your critter before letting it go. Getting an insect into a bug box isn't always easy. Try steering it in with a soft paintbrush.

Dragonflies

Fast-flying hunting insects with long bodies and clear wings that stick out sideways when they land.

Golden-ringed dragonfly (80mm long)

Identification: Our biggest dragonfly. Bright green eyes and black-and-yellow bands right up its body.

Behaviour: Often flying lazily over the streams where it lays its eggs, but also seen over heathlands. Sometimes it flies quite high, but its distinctive colours make it easy to spot.

Fact: The larva can live in a stream, mainly buried with only its head sticking out waiting for food to wander past, for up to five years before hatching as an adult dragonfly.

Where to see it: Anywhere in north, west or south Britain with acid soils. Heathlands and moorlands with shallow streams are favoured. Look for adults in your summer holidays.

Don't confuse with: This is the only dragonfly with this pattern, but there are other big blue or green ones.

Emperor dragonfly (78mm long)

Identification: A big and bulky-looking dragonfly, often looking a little droopy in flight. Both sexes have green bodies, but males have blue tails and females have green. Both have a black stripe down the tail.

Behaviour: Very powerful and always active. You won't see them perched often because they even eat in mid-air. Expect to see them zooming around over larger ponds, lakes and canals all summer.

Fact: This dragonfly defends a feeding territory against others of the same species, so you often see fights between rival males.

Where to see it: Over any large freshwater body in England, Wales and southern Scotland.

Don't confuse with: Similar hawker dragonflies. None of these have the black stripe running down their tail section.

Damselflies

Smaller, slow-motion dragonflies, with wings that lie along their body when they rest.

Common blue damselfly (33mm long)

Identification: Males are bright blue with less black than other similar species. Females may be either bright blue or dull green.

Behaviour: Flies over any lake, reservoir or pond in search of smaller insects to eat and other common blues to mate with.

Fact: This is the most common damselfly. Sometimes you can see hundreds of them together, but don't worry. They are completely harmless to people.

Where to see it: Over still water of almost any size through the UK, from May to October.

Don't confuse with: Other very similar damselflies, including azure damselfly, but this is the bluest of them all.

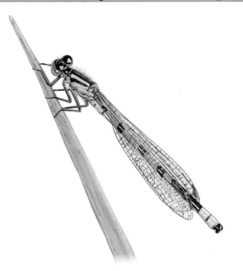

Banded agrion (48mm long)

Identification: The males of this large damselfly have a dark band through their wings that makes them flicker in flight. Females are metallic green and have dusky wings.

Behaviour: The males defend territories along slow-moving streams and canals, but sometimes group together and dance to impress females.

Fact: This damselfly can be found in suitable habitats right across the world to China.

Where to see it: Mainly slow rivers and canals with muddy bottoms throughout the UK. You rarely see it far from water.

Don't confuse with: Other green female damsels, which all have clear wings. The males' wing bars are unique.

Butterflies and moths

Butterflies and moths are all part of the group called Lepidoptera, which just means 'scaled wings'. Their wings are covered with tiny, powdery scales that give them colour. In time some of these wear off, giving older ones a tatty appearance.

About butterflies and moths

All butterflies and moths go through the same life cycle: they start as an egg, from which a caterpillar hatches out. This grows until it turns into a pupa, often called a chrysalis, which finally hatches as a flying adult which mates and lays more eggs. How long all this takes and what each creature does at these different stages of its life cycle is what makes the group interesting. Some butterflies and moths spend the winter as adults, for example, but others do so as eggs. Some moth caterpillars eat so much that they don't need to feed at all as adults, and some adult moths don't even have mouth parts at all!

All our butterflies are active during the daytime in spring or summer. Most moths come out on summer nights. However, there are more day-flying moths than there are butterflies in the UK, and you can see moths in every month of the year.

About 95% of Lepidoptera are moths. These range from the tiniest micro-moths that spend most of their life cycle inside leaves, to huge hawk moths that are bigger than any of our butterflies. Butterflies are simply one group on the scale from micro-moths to macro-moths.

Butterfly or moth?

To tell the difference between moths and butterflies in the UK is easier than in many parts of the world. All our butterflies are day-flying. They nearly all have small knobs on the ends of their antennae, unlike moths. They also don't have the little hooks that link a moth's front and hind wings together, called the frenulum. This makes their flight look stronger.

In a good butterfly garden in southern England, you may see 10 or more species in a day. That same garden could have over 100 different moths at night. If you want to get into learning about Lepidoptera, moths are the more interesting challenge!

This painted lady has typical butterfly antennae.

Looking at moths and butterflies

If you are going out looking for butterflies don't forget to look for day-flying moths as well. Of course most moths come out only at night, but that doesn't mean you can't see them. All you have to do is to learn how to bring them in.

Light

Many moths come to light, so can be attracted by leaving a bright light on – if you leave a bathroom window open on a warm, preferably damp summer's night, you will probably find moths inside in the morning (they are easier to find in the bathroom than among the soft furnishing of your bedroom). However, for best results you need a proper moth trap. These emit a lot of ultraviolet light as well as visible light, and this is not only especially attractive to moths but also less annoying for neighbours. There are moth enthusiasts all over the country who run moth trapping events at nature reserves. See if you can go along – you will have a great time.

Honeysuckle flowers smell sweetly at night to attract moths like the elephant hawk.

Sugar traps

You can also attract moths to sweet sticky liquids. Either soak a bit of rope in this special recipe, or paint it straight on to a tree trunk or fence post in late summer. If you are lucky, it will attract lots of moths that you can then have a look at. Some of the moths that come to sugar rarely come to light, so you could do this at the same time as putting a light trap out.

Recipe
- 300ml of liquid – preferably beer or red wine, but cola can also work
- 1kg soft brown sugar
- 0.5kg black treacle

Method
Boil all the ingredients together for five minutes until all the sugar has dissolved. Ask an adult to help. Stir all the time and then keep stirring as you let the mixture cool. When it is cold, either paint the mixture on to tree trunks, or soak lengths of cotton rope into it and hang them on trees. Keep watching as night falls.

Once your moths are in, gently encourage them to enter a small tube (yes, they will be able to breathe for hours) to get a closer look and identify them.

Day-flying moths and butterflies can also be kept in tubes, but you need to catch them first. A butterfly net has a long enough bag so that when you catch the insect with a flick of the wrist the insect is trapped in the bottom of the bag. Remember to let them go again when you've had a good look!

Binoculars

Close-focusing binoculars will be useful for watching insects, plus you can see those butterflies that rarely come down from the tree tops, such as white admirals, purple emperors and purple hairstreaks.

Look for gatekeeper butterflies resting with open wings.

Creep up slowly to see a red admiral butterfly well.

Butterflies

Summer jewels that brighten our countryside, parks and gardens.

Holly blue (about 30mm wingspan)

Identification: Pale blue both above and below, with darker tipped front wings especially in the female.

Behaviour: Flies higher than other blue butterflies.

Fact: Spring caterpillars eat holly, but the next generation later in the summer eats ivy.

Where to see it: Throughout England but rarer in other UK countries. Look around holly trees and hedges, in gardens, churchyards and hedgerows.

Don't confuse with: Common blue, which is a paler blue and has a darker underwing with more brown and black spots. There are several other blue butterflies in the UK.

Orange-tip (about 45mm wingspan)

Identification: Quite small for a white butterfly. Male has really bright orange wingtips. The female doesn't but both have beautiful green pattern under the wings.

Behaviour: One of the first butterflies to hatch from a pupa each year, so this is a real sign of spring. Watch it flying along country lanes and hedgerows and laying eggs on cuckooflower and garlic mustard.

Fact: Females taste plants with their feet to sense whether they will be suitable places for their eggs.

Where to see it: Country lanes, woodland rides and road verges throughout the UK.

Don't confuse with: Green-veined white and brimstone butterflies, which are flying around the same time, but neither has the bright orange wing tips.

Gatekeeper (about 40mm wingspan)

Identification: A golden brown butterfly of summer, with a dark spot in the centre of the upperwing.

Behaviour: Defends a small territory, often around a bramble bush, but flies to rough grassland to lay its eggs.

Fact: Only males have the brown band on the centre of the forewing.

Where to see it: Throughout England and Wales, but rarer in Scotland and Northern Ireland. Look for it in July and August where there are flowers for adults to feed on and long grass for them to lay eggs on. Field and woodland edges are good spots.

Don't confuse with: Meadow brown, which is larger, and the fritillaries, which are more ginger and patterned.

Painted lady (about 65mm wingspan)

Identification: A large, strong-flying orange butterfly with black and white wingtips and camouflaged underwings.

Behaviour: Spring sightings will be butterflies that have flown here from North Africa! These will breed on thistles or nettles before their offspring head south.

Fact: Though they can't survive our cold winter in any stage of their life cycle, this butterfly has even been found as far north as Iceland.

Where to see it: Anywhere! If there is an influx of painted ladies, they will turn up in any habitat all over the UK.

Don't confuse with: Red admiral and small tortoiseshell, which may be on the same bushes, but the former is red and black and the latter has a fringe of blue spots around its hindwing.

Micro-moths

Tiny and neglected, these little creatures are well worth a look.

Horse chestnut leafminer (5mm wingspan)

Identification: Adults are beautiful shiny gold with white stripes.

Behaviour: Caterpillars burrow into horse chestnut leaves and spend their whole time inside. A tree infected with horse chestnut leaf miners can have thousands and may look like autumn in the middle of summer.

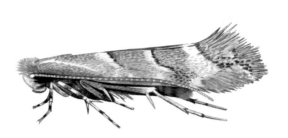

Fact: This moth was new to science in 1984, but has now spread right across England and has been found in all other UK countries as well since first being seen in London in 2002.

Where to see it: Find horse chestnut (conker) trees and keep checking during the summer until you find the moths under leaves. There may be three broods each summer, so you should find them sooner or later.

Don't confuse with: There are 34 species in the same family! This is best identified by finding it on the right tree.

Small magpie moth (25mm wingspan)

Identification: Black and white chequer-board pattern with an orange head. Often seen in daylight.

Behaviour: Will come to lit windows or moth traps, but also easily disturbed from long grass.

Fact: The caterpillar eats stinging nettles and other weeds, which is why this moth is quite common.

Where to see it: Anywhere in England, especially in the south, but rarer in Wales and Scotland. Look along country hedgerows.

Don't confuse with: Marbled white butterfly and large magpie moth, which are both much bigger, even though this is quite large for a micro-moth!

Larger moths

The hidden gems of your garden wildlife. Also called macro-moths.

Elephant hawk (50mm wingspan)

Identification: Adult moth is a large and beautiful combination of green and pink. The caterpillar is finger length and thick, either green or brown with a soft ' spike' at the tail end.

Behaviour: Caterpillars eat rosebay willowherb and the adults visit night-scented flowers to suck nectar.

Fact: It gets its name because the caterpillar is said to look like an elephant's trunk.

Where to see it: Throughout the UK. It comes readily to light from June to September, but you may see it around honeysuckle or on buddleia by torchlight.

Don't confuse with: The small elephant hawk moth, which is even pinker, but also smaller and rarer.

Angle-shades (45mm wingspan)

Identification: The wings look as if they have been creased longways, making it look like a dry leaf. The dark triangle on the wings is always present, but the whole moth can look either green or brown.

Behaviour: This moth can have two generations in a single summer, so can be found at any time of year, even though it is most common in the summer.

Fact: The caterpillar isn't too fussy. It will eat all sorts of plants, from nettles and oak leaves to dock plants and celery.

Where to see it: Comes readily to light and sugar all over the UK, but its camouflage makes it hard to spot when resting during the day.

Don't confuse with: The small angle shades, which is smaller, darker brown, less wrinkled and less common. Watch out though, there are 2500 different moths in the UK!

Garden carpet (20mm wingspan)

Identification: Usually black and white and sitting flat on a wall. Check where the black spots are carefully. Caterpillar may be either green or brown.

Behaviour: Caterpillars move in a looping movement rather than wriggling (imagine walking on all fours with your hands and feet tied!) Easily disturbed from garden plants.

Fact: Garden carpet moths are in the geometer family. This means 'ground measuring' and reflects the movement of the caterpillars.

Where to see it: As the name suggest, this is a common moth in gardens. It can be found throughout the summer all over the UK, coming to light or sugar.

Don't confuse with: Many similar species of geometer, including over 160 close relatives.

Buff arches (35-40mm wingspan)

Identification: Delicate combination of browns and greys, with fantastic wavy lines near the end of the wings make this one of our prettiest moths, especially seen under a hand lens.

Behaviour: The caterpillar eats bramble leaves and the adult moth comes to light and sugar in woodland and gardens.

Fact: These moths can hear bats coming and drop out of the sky to avoid being eaten.

Where to see it: Found throughout England, Wales and Northern Ireland, but rare in Scotland.

Don't confuse with: There are 15 species in this family. The whole family also looks similar to an even bigger family called the noctuids.

Grasshoppers and crickets

Long-legged jumpers that sing in the late summer.

Field grasshopper (18-24mm long)

Identification: Can be green or brown, but always with long, strong back legs and antennae that are shorter than its body.

Behaviour: Despite being best known for jumping, these can be quite strong flyers. You may see them sunning on walls or paths, but you can also hear their 'chirp chirp chirp' call.

Fact: Grasshoppers have ears on their back ends.

Where to see it: In summer and autumn in long grass or nearby paths and walls in the sun.

Don't confuse with: 11 different grasshoppers live in the UK.

Roesel's bush-cricket (15-25mm long)

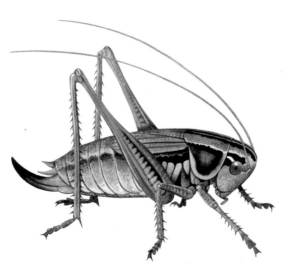

Identification: Usually brown and with pale spots along its side, just behind a big pale U-shaped mark. Very long antennae.

Behaviour: Sings loudly from long grass from June to September. The song is a long, continuous high-pitched hiss, above the hearing of many adults.

Fact: It used to live in southern England, but is rapidly spreading north and west.

Where to see it: In long grass, meadows and unkempt road verges right across lowland England and surely soon in the rest of the UK.

Don't confuse with: The very long antennae and, on females, the long curved egg-laying tube (it's not a stinger) help tell bush crickets from grasshoppers, but there are 10 species in the UK.

Ants, wasps and bees

Narrow-waisted insects that reveal the three-part body plan: head, thorax and abdomen.

Southern wood ant (8mm long)

Identification: This is a very big, dark red-brown ant that lives in huge colonies in open pine woods.

Behaviour: You can watch ants for days as they work together for the sake of their colony, which is a huge heap of pine needles.

Fact: A big wood ant colony can collect and bring back over 60,000 food items every day.

Where to see it: In open woodland in southern England and Wales. Look for big heaps (several buckets full) of pine needles crawling with ants, or follow trails of ants that you see crossing woodland tracks.

Don't confuse with: Garden ants. The three species of wood ants in the UK are much larger.

Wood wasp (4cm long)

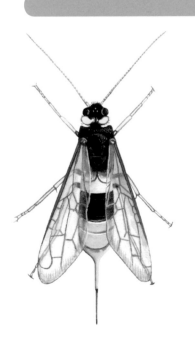

Identification: Big, fierce-looking, but completely harmless black and yellow wasp. Female has a long spike sticking out of its back end. It's not a sting; it's an egg-laying tube.

Behaviour: Uses its long egg-laying tube (called an ovipositor) to lay its eggs deep inside rotting wood. The grub eats the wood inside until it hatches out two years later.

Fact: The female may take as long as 15 minutes to drill a hole through the bark of a tree to lay her egg in the hard wood beneath.

Where to see it: Never common, but in woods and gardens throughout the UK. Occasionally hatches from timber in houses so may be seen against the window – be brave and let it out!

Don't confuse with: Hornets, which are fatter, more like huge browner wasps. There are perhaps 150 different sawflies in the UK, but this is the biggest.

113

Ruby-tailed jewel wasp (12mm long)

Identification: Bright metallic turquoise head and body and shiny red tail. This is smaller than garden wasps and usually seen on its own.

Behaviour: Tracks down other solitary wasps and lays its eggs in their nests where it will eat their larvae.

Fact: Jewel wasps are usually noticed only in bright sunshine and are sometimes called cuckoo wasps. They don't sting.

Where to see it: On heathlands and in gardens throughout the UK. Look for other solitary wasps and bees and you may see this nearby, perhaps feeding on pollen in flowers.

Don't confuse with: There are other similar species, but this is the most commonly seen.

Buff-tailed bumblebee (1.5-2.5cm long)

Identification: One of the classic hairy, black and yellow bumblebees. Queens are biggest and have buff tails. The smaller workers come out later in the year. They have white tails.

Behaviour: Queens emerge first in the spring and build a small nest which may contain up to 300 bees by late summer.

Where to see it: In gardens, parks, hedgerows and flower meadows across the UK, and earlier in the spring than many species.

Don't confuse with: White-tailed bumblebee, which is a bit smaller and even the queen has a white tail. There are around 25 bumblebee species in the UK and far more lone mining bees.

Flies

Flies have just two main flight wings whereas bees, butterflies and moths have four.

Flesh-fly (15mm long)

Identification: Quite large and harmless flies, usually with red eyes and with pale stripes or a chequer-board pattern running along the body.

Behaviour: Females lay their eggs or living maggots on dead and rotting animals. Some even lay eggs in open wounds on living animals! The adult flies suck up all sorts of sugary and meaty liquids.

Fact: Their life cycle is so predictable that forensic scientists can tell when a dead body died by examining the flesh-flies living on them.

Where to see it: Found across the UK, but rarely indoors. You will see plenty of them on any dead animal you come across.

Don't confuse with: Picture-wing and horse flies look similar but often have multi-coloured eyes – and they bite!

Greater bee-fly (14-18mm long)

Identification: Brown and furry like a small bumblebee, but with a long proboscis sticking out of the front of its face.

Behaviour: Hovers perfectly still in mid-air above woodland glades and tracks, and visits spring flowers such as primroses to take nectar.

Fact: Not only does this look like a bee, but its young eat bees. The mother bee-fly flicks her eggs towards the entrance holes of solitary bees. When the maggots hatch out, they crawl into the bee's home and start eating its larvae!

Where to see it: Found across the UK and usually seen from March to May.

Don't confuse with: Its long legs, sticky-out proboscis and hovering flight help to tell this apart from the bees.

St Mark's fly (12-14mm long)

Identification: Males are slow-moving, hairy black flies with long dangly legs that dance at around head height in the spring. The females are a little larger and with smaller eyes. They will be perched on leaves nearby watching.

Behaviour: Adult males live for around a week, during which time they are completely focused on finding mates. The females will mate, lay eggs underground and then die. For most of the year, this fly exists only as wriggling larvae.

Fact: The fly is named after its supposed hatching date. St Mark's Day is 25 April.

Where to see it: Over rough grassland, woodland rides and hedgerows across the UK.

Don't confuse with: This is one of 20 species in the same family, and there are over 7,000 flies in the UK, but this is the one you are most likely to notice.

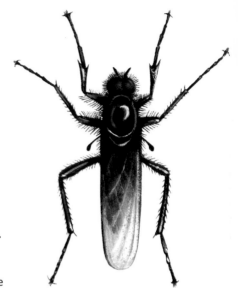

Marmalade hoverfly (10mm)

Identification: Much smaller than wasps, with orange and black bands across its abdomen and fainter stripes along its thorax. Hovers a lot, but also visits garden flowers.

Behaviour: The larvae eat aphids, but the adults visit flowers for nectar and pollen. Males can be seen hovering in sunny spots. They will be defending a territory near an aphid colony.

Fact: The UK sometimes get huge influxes of these from abroad. These tiny insects can fly here from across the sea!

Where to see it: Across the UK in gardens, woodlands and hedgerows. Expect greater numbers after spring and late summer migrations.

Don't confuse with: Wasps! Hoverflies don't sting and there are over 250 species in the UK.

Bugs

In America, all minibeasts are known as bugs, but true bugs all have piercing mouthparts to suck up food.

Hawthorn shield bug (17mm long)

Identification: Yes, shield bugs are shaped like shields! This one is green and brown with dull red eyes.

Behaviour: Uses its mouthparts like a straw to suck juices from hawthorn berries and leaves, but often remains well hidden and slow moving.

Fact: These bugs are sometimes called stink bugs. Now see if you can find one to discover why!

Where to see it: Hawthorn bushes and even oak trees throughout the UK have these camouflaged insects hiding in them. You will most likely see one that has been surprised out in the open.

Don't confuse with: The shape will help you identify shield bugs but there are about 45 species in the UK.

Rhododendron leafhopper (11mm long)

Identification: The scarlet stripes on a green background make this one of our most recognisable leafhoppers.

Behaviour: Sucks sap from within rhododendron leaves. Quite approachable, but will hop away with a click of its back legs if you get too close.

Fact: This is one of the very few insects that eat rhododendron.

Where to see it: Look in late summer on rhododendron leaves, mainly in southern England.

Don't confuse with: The shape makes this clearly a leafhopper, but if you find one of a different colour beware. There are over 400 other species to choose from!

Stilt bug (12-18mm long)

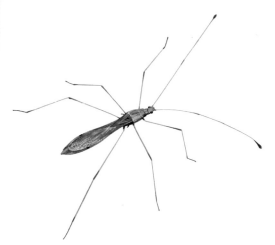

Identification: All 100 or so species have very long legs and long antennae. They are often camouflaged against the leaves they live on, being usually plain green, brown or grey.

Behaviour: They walk slowly along the plant leaves and stems, and often freeze if they think they have been spotted.

Fact: Although stilt bugs eat plant juices, they have relatives, such as the assassin bugs, that hunt other insects and suck them dry!

Where to see them: You can find stilt bugs in many different habitats, but one of the easiest ways is to go tree-beating.

Don't confuse with: Other than the other 99 stilt bugs, don't mistake this for a spider – it only has six legs.

Pond skater (12-15mm long)

Identification: A grey bug scooting over a pond surface, with its body raised up on long legs will be a pond skater.

Behaviour: Often waits at the edges of the pond, detecting the vibrations of a dying insect that has fallen in. Then it uses its middle legs to skate out, pierce the hapless victim with its beak and suck it dry. Lovely!

Fact: Pond skaters have water-repellent hairs on their feet to help them glide on the water's surface tension.

Where to see them: Any pond will have pond skaters, but quieter ones without fish will be best. You can see these insects on mild days, even late into the autumn and early in spring.

Don't confuse with: There are seven similar species in the UK, along with water-measurers. These move much more slowly and look gangly compared with pond skaters.

Beetles

One of the most interesting and diverse groups of insects, but tricky to identify.

Click beetle (9-13mm long)

Identification: A long, slim beetle, pale brown with its head and thorax sunken. Close up, its antennae are jointed.

Behaviour: The larvae are grubs that live under the bark of all sorts of trees. Adults can be found feeding on pollen in garden flowers and on trees.

Fact: If you hold one, it may flex its body quickly to right itself or escape. This is the 'click' that gives these beetles their name.

Where to see it: Through the UK, in the summer on garden flowers and in woodlands, often in your sheet after tree-beating.

Don't confuse with: There are 73 different click beetles in the UK, mostly plain browns or black.

Devil's coach-horse (25-30mm)

Identification: Large, flexible black beetle, a bit like a giant earwig.

Behaviour: Voracious predator that isn't afraid to turn on people and give them a nip, but more usually it arches its tail in threat, perhaps imitating a scorpion.

Fact: When threatened, it can release a foul-smelling white fluid that may stop small mammals attacking it.

Where to see it: It usually hides under logs or stones in the daytime and comes out to hunt at night. You are most likely to see one running across a footpath or perhaps in a pitfall trap – when it may have eaten anything else that fell into the same trap.

Don't confuse with: This is one of around 1,000 rove beetles in the UK, but its size marks it out. Earwigs are much smaller and brown.

Common red soldier beetle (12-15mm long)

Identification: A slim mainly dull orange beetle with a black tail end. Often seen in pairs.

Behaviour: The larvae spend most of their time on the ground hunting for smaller creatures to eat. The adults survive for only a few weeks and spend much of their time mating.

Fact: Many children call these bloodsuckers, but soldier beetles are completely harmless to humans.

Where to see it: Across the UK, in parks, gardens, meadows and woodland rides.

Don't confuse with: There are around 40 different soldier beetles in the UK.

Cockchafer (up to 30mm long)

Identification: Large, blundering brown summer beetle, with whirring flight and fantastic branched antennae.

Behaviour: Flies from dusk in May and June and can be very common in some places. If one lands on your clothing, it can grip surprisingly strongly, but they are harmless and generally slow-moving.

Fact: Cockchafer grubs can live in the soil for up to four years before hatching as adults.

Where to see it: Across the UK, in gardens, parks and woodland edges. The adults favour broad-leaved trees.

Don't confuse with: Other chafers, which are smaller or more brightly coloured, but we have around 4,000 beetles in the UK.

Other insects

We can't cover all the 20,000 insects in the UK, but here are a couple of lovely oddities.

Silverfish (15-20mm)

Identification: Imagine a shiny, fast moving cross between a centipede and a woodlouse and you have a silverfish. No wings, three tails and long antennae help.

Behaviour: They come out at night and pick up leftovers from crumbs and dead insects to glue and cardboard.

Fact: Silverfish have been around since the time of the dinosaurs.

Where to see it: Usually indoors on hard surfaces. They prefer damp and unheated homes. Look in old bathrooms or under your kitchen sink, or in old church corners.

Don't confuse with: Marine bristletails, found under seaweedy rocks above the high-water mark on beaches right around our coasts. They are much larger.

Moorhen flea (2mm long)

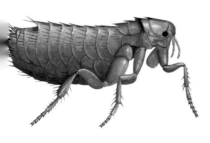

Identification: Fleas are all small, slippery, wingless and shiny with huge back legs. They are flattened so that they can run through fur and feathers with ease.

Behaviour: They bite to drink blood as food and mostly crawl slowly along. The famous flea jump is for getting from one host animal or its nest to another.

Fact: Moorhen fleas tend to stay on the bird (not just moorhens!) but may also live in old nests. If you find a freshly dead bird, its fleas will be trying to escape as the body cools down.

Where to see it: Different creatures have different sorts of flea. For bird fleas this often depends on the sort of nest the bird makes.

Don't confuse with: If you can keep them still, types of fleas look different under a magnifying glass. They may be different colours and sizes and some have arched backs where others have rounded backs.

Other minibeasts – spiders

Eight legs, eight eyes, poison fangs and neither wings nor antennae – spiders are perfect little hunters. They don't all spin webs.

Zebra spider (5-7mm)

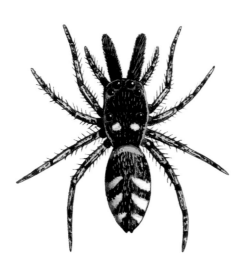

Identification: Black-and-white striped, with two bigger forward-facing eyes to help it judge its distance from its prey.

Behaviour: Creeps up on prey its own size in a jerky fashion, then jumps on the insect. If you get too close, it will probably turn to have a look at you – don't worry, it's harmless to people.

Fact: Jumping spiders fix themselves a safety line of silk before they jump – so they can climb back up if they miss their target.

Where to see it: Window frames, sunny walls and garden fences in the summer are easiest, but you can also find them stalking insects on tree trunks.

Don't confuse with: There are other jumping spiders, but this one is quite distinctive.

Fen raft spider (up to 70mm leg span)

Identification: Our biggest spider. Chocolate brown with a pale cream stripe along its side. As with other spiders, the female is much bigger than the male.

Behaviour: Waits at the edge of ponds with its front legs on the water surface. When it feels a ripple, it rushes out across the water surface to grab its prey. But also hunts by swimming under water.

Fact: Despite being big enough to catch small fish, this spider was only first noticed in Britain in the 1950s.

Where to see it: This spider lives in ponds in bogs and reedbed pools but in only a few places nowadays. Conservationists are breeding them to release in new areas to help the species survive.

Don't confuse with: The common house spider is the huge hairy beast that runs across your floor, but there are 600 other types of spider in the UK.

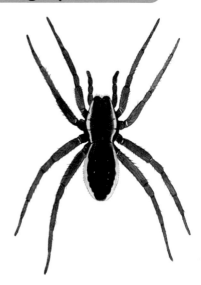

Daddy long-legs spider

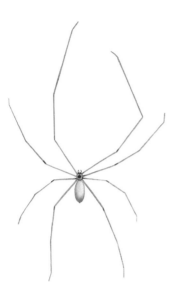

Identification: Very long thin legs that make it look more like a daddy long legs than a normal spider.

Behaviour: Hangs upside-down in a rather feeble web in the corner of a room, waiting to go hunting at night. If you disturb it, the spider will vibrate its web so quickly that it becomes almost invisible.

Fact: The long legs of this spider help keep dangerous prey, such as other spiders, at arm's length while it is bundling them up in silk.

Where to see it: Look in the high corners of rooms, especially in southern Britain. Even though this is a wild animal, you won't find one outdoors because it can't cope with the cold.

Don't confuse with: Real daddy long-legs have two wings and six legs.

Woodlouse spider

Identification: The pale reddish brown body and huge fangs make this unmistakeable. It is not as quick moving as many of our spiders so you have plenty of time to get a closer look.

Behaviour: During the day, this spider stays under dry stones in a silk bed, but comes out at night to hunt its favourite prey – woodlice.

Fact: Most of our spiders don't have jaws strong enough to bite people, but this one does because it is adapted for crunching through woodlice.

Where to see it: They sometimes come into houses, but you are more likely to find one under a brick in your garden.

Don't confuse with: One other similar species, but it is much rarer.

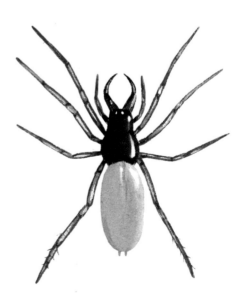

Crustaceans

There are so many different types of crustacean that ways to look at one won't help much when you look at another. What works for studying woodlice (such as looking under stones in your garden) won't work for looking at lobsters in the sea!

However, there are similarities that may help. Crustaceans have 10 jointed legs, and they are likely to want to get away before you can study them. In general, they are shy, live in holes and most eat anything they can catch. This means that you will have to go looking in holes, often at night and that you can sometimes tempt them out with tasty titbits.

The obvious example here is crabbing. To catch crabs and have a look at them, you need a fishing line with a bit of bait on the end – usually meat or fish – and then somewhere that crabs live. Piers and rockpools are good places. To avoid hurting the crab, rather than attach your bait with a hook, you could tie it on, perhaps in a little mesh bag – such as an emptied teabag. The crabs will be so keen that you can haul them up still clinging on to their food!

Woodlice

Most crustaceans, including crabs, lobsters, prawns and barnacles are marine creatures, but woodlice live on the land. You may even find them indoors, where they come out at night to look for scraps. However, you are more likely to find them under plant pots in a greenhouse, in the shed or under logs and stones.

There are 40 species of woodlice in the UK, but some of them are very rare. The more common ones are easy to study in an old fish tank. Keep them for a few days and find out where they prefer to live. Will they go to the damp or dry spots?

Woodlice have lots of old country names including cheesy bug, rolypoly and chuggypig!

Most crustaceans live in water. There may be over 70,000 different types worldwide.

Acorn barnacle (up to 15mm across)

Identification: Acorn barnacles are the small white or pale brown shell-like cones that cling to seashore rocks and shellfish, and that stop you slipping into the waves.

Behaviour: Acorn barnacles spend their whole adult lives clinging to the same rock or shell. They open their shells and wave their feet out of the top to look for food.

Fact: Baby barnacles drift through the sea as part of the plankton, but once they choose a surface to settle on, they stick there for life.

Where to see it: On rocks, sea defences and on the backs of crabs and shells all around the coast in the intertidal zone.

Don't confuse with: The diamond-shaped opening (as opposed to oval or round) helps to set this apart from other species.

Water flea (less than 2mm across)

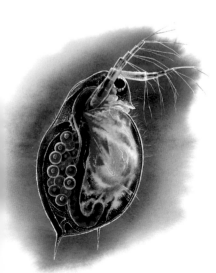

Identification: The tiniest creatures that you are likely to be able to see. Water fleas are mostly see-through, and move through the water in a skipping motion.

Behaviour: Skips through the water in search of even tinier things to eat, such as bacteria and tiny plants.

Fact: Water fleas are the first animals on many food chains. Without water fleas there would be no otters or kingfishers.

Where to see it: Hold a glass of pond or river water up to the light, and look for little jumpers. You will need a microscope to have a proper look.

Don't confuse with: There are around 80 different types of water flea in the UK, but this is among the most common. Fish shops sometimes sell bags of giant water fleas (although they are still very small!) as fish food.

Sea slater (up to 30mm long)

Identification: Like a giant grey or green woodlouse.

Behaviour: Stays hidden in a crack or under rocks and seaweeds on rocky shores during the day. Comes out at night to find all sorts of things to eat.

Fact: Sea slaters can live for up to three years.

Where to see it: On the upper shore right around our coast. Look under seaweed on the strand line. You will often find quite a lot together.

Don't confuse with: Other woodlice, which are much smaller and don't live on the seashore.

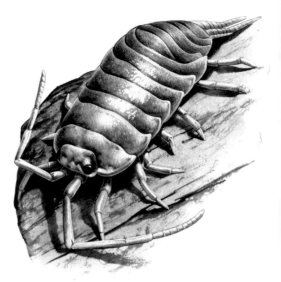

Lobster (up to 50cm long)

Identification: Huge claws, bluish shell, 10 pairs of legs and a flattened body. This is a sea species. Crayfish in some of our lakes and rivers have similar body plans but are much smaller.

Behaviour: Lobsters live in holes in rocks in shallow seas and come out to catch fish and other creatures, dead or alive.

Fact: Wild lobsters can live for more than 15 years, as long as they aren't caught by people.

Where to see it: Lobsters live below the low tide line, so you are most likely to see one as part of a fishing boat's catch.

Don't confuse with: There is only one species of lobster in UK seas, and its shape should stop you confusing it with anything else.

Molluscs

Nearly a quarter of all known sea creatures are molluscs. There are plenty living on land and in freshwater as well. They range from octopuses and giant squids, to limpets, oysters, slugs and snails. It can be quite hard to decide what is and isn't a mollusc!

Most have shells, but not all. Most eat plants, but not all. And most prefer damp or wet places to live, but again, not all. Most are slow moving by human standards, especially the land molluscs, but others, such as cuttlefish, are fast moving. Some barely see the world at all through tiny eyes, but others have eyes that are every bit as good as our own.

Looking at molluscs

Molluscs can be studied alive or dead. By dead, I mean by collecting seashells or investigating whether particular colours of snail shell are more common on song thrush anvils than others.

Watching living land molluscs and even many of those at the seaside is all about knowing where to look. Start with damp places – under logs and stones, in ponds or rockpools.

When you find a snail or slug that has curled up and hidden away from the drying sun, you can often coax it out to get a decent look by splashing it with fresh water (or seawater for molluscs you find on the beach). Give it a little time to detect the water and the creature may come out to see what's going on.

Find mussels below the high water line at the seaside.

Leopard slug (up to 20cm long)

Identification: A huge and attractive slug with bold black and white stripes on the tail and leopard spotting on its back.

Behaviour: These slugs mate for hours while hanging from a sticky rope that they make.

Fact: This is one of the biggest slugs in the world!

Where to see it: Always near humans, perhaps in a damp cellar or wet corner of an outhouse where it can eat mouldy wood.

Don't confuse with: There are around 30 different slugs in the UK, but this is the biggest you are likely to see.

Banded snail (shell up to 20mm tall)

Identification: A medium-sized snail with lovely swirls of brown, cream, white or yellow, spiralling round the shell.

Behaviour: Only active in the spring and summer. They hibernate all winter.

Fact: These snails' patterns help them avoid being seen by their arch enemy, the song thrush.

Where to see them: Very common in grassland throughout the UK.

Don't confuse with: There are two similar species, one with a pale lip to the shell and one with a dark lip.

Shellfish

Shells provide protection for these seaside molluscs.

Blue-rayed limpet (up to 15mm across)

Identification: Oval, amber coloured but see-through shell with lines of bright electric blue spots.

Behaviour: Blue-rayed limpets cling to and graze the seaweed just below the low-water mark, especially on rough coasts.

Fact: You find the biggest and oldest blue-rayed limpets near to the holdfast, where the seaweed clings on to its rock.

Where to see it: Look on the huge oarweed seaweed at the lowest of tides, either in rockpools or by snorkelling over them. They can sometimes be found still clinging to seaweed that's been washed up on the beach after a storm.

Don't confuse with: The other limpets, which are much larger, live higher up the beach and don't have the electric blue bling!

Edible or blue mussel (up to 10cm long)

Identification: Purple, blue, black or sometimes brown, with two shells that mirror one another. Usually in clumps of hundreds together.

Behaviour: Mussels are filter feeders. This means they suck sea water in, filter out tiny particles to eat and then squirt the remaining water out again. That's why you never see open mussels above the water line.

Fact: Mussels can work together to tie down predatory whelks with strong threads that they grow.

Where to see it: Mussels occur around all our coasts. The easiest places to see them are stuck on the wooden posts of piers and harbours – or at your local supermarket fish counter.

Don't confuse with: This is the only bivalve – two-shelled animal – of this size and colour.

Other animals

We can't cover everything in the one small book, but we couldn't leave these out!

Centipede (up to 5cm long)

Identification: Usually red or brown with a single pair of legs for each segment. Looks like it has been flattened.

Behaviour: Lives under logs and stones, but may come out at night. A keen hunter of smaller creatures.

Fact: Despite centipede meaning 100 feet, ours rarely have more than 30.

Where to see it: Under stones and logs throughout the UK.

Don't confuse with: Millipedes, which have two pairs of legs per body segment and look much rounder when seen head-on.

Medicinal leech (up to 20cm long)

Identification: A big, stretchy, dark, worm-like creature, often with green or orange stripes running down it.

Behaviour: Feeds by attaching itself to an animal and sucking blood. Their slinky movement is fantastic.

Fact: Doctors used to bleed people with leeches to try to remove blood poisons. It didn't work.

Where to see it: They are now quite rare, but found throughout Britain in muddy ponds.

Don't confuse with: Many much smaller leeches, which live in ponds.

Soil mites (microscopic – under 1mm long)

Identification: Soil mites are tiny and often white. You will need a good hand lens or microscope to see one well. When you do so, it will probably have a rounded body and eight tiny little legs.

Behaviour: They spend their time eating even tinier creatures, such as soil bacteria, and trying not to be eaten themselves.

Fact: If you lie down on the grass, you will have more soil mites beneath you than there are people on the planet!

Where to see it: Under a microscope near you – all soil has mites.

Don't confuse with: Soil mites are slow moving, unlike the primitive bouncing springtail insects that you may also see in soil.

Dead-man's fingers (up to 250mm tall)

Identification: A soft coral that looks like it has fingers sticking out of the colony. It is often white, but may be brown or orange.

Behaviour: It sticks its tentacles out into the strong current to catch tiny animals that are swept past.

Fact: Colonies of dead man's fingers are usually either all male or all female, but all the colonies in an area release their eggs together.

Where to see it: At the very low-water line down to 100m below water, all around our coasts.

Don't confuse with: Other soft corals and sponges.

Common brittle star (up to 50mm across)

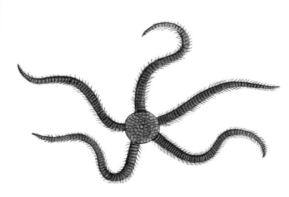

Identification: Round grey or brown body with five bristly legs that look as though they have been stuck on.

Behaviour: Usually seen moving very slowly in a rocky or sandy tidal pool, when it will be feeding on tiny creatures or anything else that drifts by.

Fact: Brittle stars are really brittle and their arms can snap off very easily. But they can grow new ones.

Where to see it: Often overlooked, but you can find these in tidal pools right around the UK's coasts. Sometimes they bury themselves just under the sandy bottom.

Don't confuse with: There are many different brittle stars in our seas, but they all have the same body shape. Other starfish look more at one with their legs.

Sea orange sponge (up to 40cm across)

Identification: Usually orange or red, but sometimes duller brown when growing deeper in the sea. It can be a range of shapes and always has a few obvious holes in it.

Behaviour: Sponges don't move much, so if you see one of these attached to a rock don't expect it to walk off. It spends its life filtering tiny bits of food from the sea.

Fact: Despite looking more like a fungus, a sponge is a colony of tiny animals. It is said that if you put one through a blender it will re-form and carry on living, but please don't try this!

Where to see them: Low down on the shore or from harbour walls all around our coasts.

Don't confuse with: There are over 160 sponges in the UK and many of them look very different dead out of the water compared with being alive. Several are orange.

Worms and anemones

Soft-bodied, but no less successful for the lack of bones or a shell.

Earthworm (up to 25cm long)

Identification: Pinky grey worm, with paler brownish saddle near the head end – that's the end at the front when the worm is travelling along.

Behaviour: This worm digs a burrow, but comes to the surface to find dead leaves and even dead insects to drag into its home to eat.

Fact: Earthworms can live for at least six years if they don't get eaten by a robin or hedgehog.

Where to see it: This is the most common worm in lawns and is the one you are most likely to see on a pavement after rain.

Don't confuse with: There may be 3,000 different types of worms worldwide, but no one is quite sure how many live in the UK.

Strawberry sea-anemone (75mm across)

Identification: Above water, it looks like a big, green-flecked strawberry. Underwater, it spreads its ring of stinging tentacles.

Behaviour: Spends low tide just above the water under a ledge in a rockpool, spreading its tentacles when the water rises to cover it. The tentacles have stinging tips to help the anemone catch small swimming creatures to eat.

Fact: Sea anemones stick on to the rock so hard that you would hurt one trying to take it off – so please don't.

Where to see it: Low down on rocky shores in southern England.

Don't confuse with: Beadlet anemone, which is smaller, and doesn't have the green spots, but it is found around all our coasts.

Parasites

These plants and animals spend their whole lives living on or in another life form.

Tapeworm (up to 30m long, but can be smaller)

Identification: Adult tapeworms are usually white and their bodies are made up of many identical segments.

Behaviour: Adults live in the gut of their main host – bird, mammal, fish, amphibian, reptile or fish. They lay eggs in the animal's poo. These hatch and live in another creature until it is eaten by one of the main hosts, where it grows to be another adult.

Fact: Like other parasites, tapeworms rarely kill their host – after all, the host is their lifeline.

Where to see it: You probably never will unless your pet has one – they stay hidden inside other animals.

Don't confuse with: There are over 1,000 types of tapeworms and plenty of other parasites, such as the roundworms that are smooth and lack the body segments.

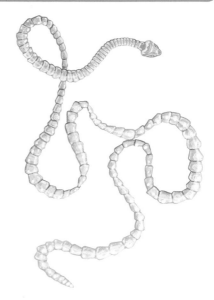

Greater dodder (stems up to 1m long)

Identification: Long, thin, red stems twining around nettle or thistle plants, but with no obvious leaves. White or pink flowers.

Behaviour: When its seeds hatch, dodder sniffs out a plant to grow towards, then attaches itself to the host and steals all its food.

Fact: In some places this parasitic plant used to be known as 'devil's guts'. Lovely!

Where to see it: Mainly in southern and eastern England, in nettlebeds, on hedgerows and river banks.

Don't confuse with: Other dodder species, which live in drier places. The lack of leaves and yellow, orange or green stems should help you be sure that you are seeing dodder.

Trees

Trees are big, easy to find and don't run away, but that doesn't make them dull or easy to identify. There is a lot to tree watching, and that's before you even start to look at what lives in them.

Looking at trees

There are five things to look for when identifying a tree, but you don't have to see them all every time.

1. Its overall size and shape – often different in summer and winter. Look for the angle of branches coming from the main trunk and how straight they are. Do this from a distance.

2. Bark and buds – is the bark smooth, deeply lined, or cracked and peeling? Is it grey or reddish brown, or even silver? And look closely at the buds, especially in winter. Their colour will help, and you may also be able to work out how the leaves are going to grow. You will be doing this from close up – the tree won't escape.

3. The size and shape of the leaves – check whether the edges are smooth or toothed, whether the whole leaf is corrugated or smooth and how big it is. Do the leaves grow in bunches or is each one very separate? Beware leaves under a tree that may have blown in from elsewhere.

4. Flowers – Some trees have very obvious spring flowers, such as horse chestnuts (conker trees). Others have little green flowers. The showy ones need to attract insects. The others have pollen that blows in the wind.

5. Fruits and nuts – From conkers to crab apples or beech nuts to pine cones, a tree's seeds are distinctive, but often don't last long – especially if a squirrel gets there first.

Look for acorns on oak trees in autumn.

How tall and how old?

Two things you may want to know about any trees you find are: how tall is it and how old is it?

How tall?

Walk away from the tree and stop. Now bend over and look back at the tree through your legs.

If you can't see the top of the tree, walk on a bit farther and try again.

When you can just see the very top of the tree through your legs, stand up.

Turn around and count the number of big paces from you to the tree, and then do the maths.

Number of paces X length of each pace in metres = height of the tree. Most people's paces are around a metre long.

The distinctive white peeling bark of silver birch will help you identify it.

How old?

Different types of tree grow at different speeds. Silver birch trees, for example, grow much quicker than yew trees. Even the same sort of trees may grow differently, depending on the soil, the rainfall and how much light they get and even whether they have been regularly pruned by people or grazing animals. However, there is an easy way to get a rough idea of how old a living tree is:

Measure all the way around the trunk of the tree about 1.3m above the ground (above the broadest part where the tree's roots spread into the ground).

Multiply this number in centimetres by 0.4 to get a rough age in years.

If you find a fresh tree stump, see if you can count the tree rings. You should find one per year that the tree grew, but they can be hard to see.

Conifer trees

Pine, fir and other conifer trees all have thin needle-like leaves. Most keep their leaves all year round.

Yew (up to 20m tall)

Identification: Dense, dark and bushy, with bright red fruit-like cones called arils. Thin leaves arranged in two flattened rows of spirals. Thin, flaky, reddish brown bark.

Fact: This tree can live for thousands of years. Most parts are poisonous to people.

Uses: Yew wood was used to make longbows in the middle ages. All parts of the tree are used in medicines, but it has also been used as a poison.

Where to see it: You will find this tree in old churchyards, and it is also used in hedges in country houses. It is hard to find in the wild now because so many were used to make bows.

Don't confuse with: Juniper, which is smaller with blue berries; Leyland cypress, which is the common, often unruly bushy tree of many garden hedges.

Scots Pine (up to 40m tall)

Identification: Long, bare straight trunk and a mass of needles on top. The needles are blue-green and grow in pairs. The cones start out red, before turning green and then brown in the two years they take to mature.

Fact: Scotland's national tree. Ancient Scots pine forests are among our most important wildlife habitats.

Uses: This tree is planted a lot for its timber and for wood pulp for making paper – perhaps even this book.

Where to see it: The Highlands in Scotland still have some native pine forest with these trees, but you can also see them planted in many places, especially where the soil is poor and sandy.

Don't confuse with: Other conifers such as Norway spruce and Douglas fir, which have a pyramidal, Christmas-tree shape.

Deciduous trees

They lose their leaves in winter as a way to save water.

Wild cherry (up to around 30m tall)

Identification: Straight trunk with dark red-brown smooth bark that flakes. Masses of white flowers come out at the same time as the leaves in early spring. Look for cherries in the summer.

Fact: Cherry trees produce cherries that birds and animals then eat. The cherry stone passes through the animal's gut. The poo acts as fertiliser for the seedling.

Uses: Cherry wood is very hard, so is a prized wood for craft workers. But did you know that cuts in cherry bark will leak a healing goo that can be used as chewing gum?

Where to see it: Throughout the UK, especially on chalky soils, and commonly on the edges of woodlands or in hedgerows because it likes more light than the centre of a wood can provide.

Don't confuse with: Smaller, pink-flowered Japanese cherries are commonly planted along suburban roadsides.

Goat willow (up to 12m tall)

Identification: One of the pussy willows, so called because of its furry-looking female flowers. Often has many stems.

Fact: Male and female trees are separate, which is why you will only see pussy willow catkins on half the trees. The wind blows the pollen between the trees, but bees also go mad for it.

Uses: Willow bark contains the active chemical in aspirin.

Where to see them: Damp open woodlands and along the banks of slow-moving rivers and canals.

Don't confuse with: There are many similar willows and hybrids which makes them very hard to identify, but the leaves and catkins will get you as far as willow tree.

Wildflowers

You can find wildflowers from early spring right through to late autumn, and even in the winter in southerly sheltered places. However, April to August is the main time to see them. Some of the earliest flowers are on woodland floors, where they aim to catch the sun and visiting insects before the tree leaves block out the light.

In May and June, hedgerows and flower meadows are at their peak, especially in the south. Later, in July and August, and farther north, the flowers of the uplands and lowland heaths bloom. The hills turn purple with heather.

There are a few flowers that only come out in autumn. This may be reflected in their names, such as the autumn gentian.

Flowers are there for one purpose: to help the plant reproduce itself. The flowers themselves may be adapted to attract butterflies, moths, bees or other flying insects, or they may be simply open to the wind.

It is usually much easier to identify the plant when it is flowering, but a few species, such as cuckoo pint, have such distinctive berries that many people notice them only in the autumn.

Primroses are much less common than they used to be.

Watching wildflowers

To study wildflowers you need patience – waiting for them to flower or to open is half the battle. Once they have done so, you will want to get a close look, so a hand lens is useful. These days, most people prefer to record their flowers by photographing them, but there is a long tradition of painting and preserving wildflowers.

Painting flowers

Botanical artists have a reputation for exactness, and a good botanical illustration can usually say more about the plant than an average photograph. However, it takes time and almost always means picking the flower and bringing it indoors. Unless you have permission, please leave wildflowers for everyone to enjoy.

Pressing flowers

Preserving flowers is usually done by pressing them. Freshly picked flowers are arranged on tissue paper and placed between two boards. They are then squashed for weeks under a heavy weight or by screwing the boards down in a proper flower press. The result usually preserves the form of the flower, but the colours tend to fade, so this technique is best combined with painting or photography.

Growing flowers

Collecting and drying the seeds of wildflowers means that you can grow them at home, especially if they are local, so the soil is similar. Collect seed pods in paper envelopes to stop the seed rotting, and store them in a shed or unheated place (away from house mice!). Plant them in the spring.

Willowherb seeds are fluffy and float on the wind to find new homes.

Wildflowers of wetlands

Wetland flowers are often quite tall because they can get all the water they need to grow.

Flag iris (up to 1.5m tall)

Identification: Very tall flower spike with a bright yellow, floppy-looking flower that has three big drooping petals and three more horizontal ones. Often grows in a clump.

Fact: Big clumps, or stands, of irises that have spread by rhizomes grow in damp corners, wetland and ponds, but the flowers also produce seeds that float away and grow into new plants when they settle.

Uses: The flowers, underground rhizomes and stems of flag irises have been used to create dyes for fabrics. Depending how they are treated, it can make yellow, green, brown or even black dyes.

Where to see it: In ditches, ponds and reedbeds throughout the UK, but the biggest iris beds are perhaps in western Scotland.

Don't confuse with: Stinking iris, which is our only other native iris and is bluey-grey. You may also encounter other species that have escaped from gardens.

Meadowsweet (up to 1.5m tall)

Identification: Paired crinkly leaves, each with three lobes on spindly, sometimes reddish stems give way to frothy white clumps of flowers that smell very sweet.

Fact: Thick mats of meadowsweet in damp meadows get full of insects.

Uses: The plant contains the chemical that aspirin is made from, and because it smells so sweet was sometimes strewn around indoors to mask dodgy smells.

Where to see it: In damp meadows, along stream banks and in damp woodland rides across the UK.

Don't confuse with: If it's growing somewhere damp and smells sweet there shouldn't be any confusion, but check out hemp agrimony as well.

Wildflowers of coasts

Low and tough plants that have to cope with salt and sea winds.

Thrift or sea pink (up to 25cm tall)

Identification: Forms cushions of very narrow leaves from which tall pompom pink flowers grow.

Fact: Can cope with dry salty ground, so you can find this growing on rocks, on sand dunes, or on grassland all around the coast.

Uses: Possibly because its growth is adapted to conserve water, it is associated with saving money, which maybe why it used to feature on the threepenny coin that was used in the UK until 1971.

Where to see it: Anywhere around the coast, but perhaps at its best in the western isles of Scotland.

Don't confuse with: Other pink coastal flowers, such as centaury and wild thyme. But they don't have the same combination of a cushion of leaves and tall flower stems.

Yellow horned poppy (up to 90cm tall)

Identification: Four bright yellow petals grow from pale, icy green clumps. The seed pods can be 30cm long and are very thin. They look a bit like horns, hence the name.

Fact: Only found naturally growing on coastal shingle beaches, where it can help to hold the beach together, but also grows on railway tracks.

Uses: Yellow horned poppy is poisonous to people, but may have medicinal uses.

Where to see it: It's quite sensitive to disturbance and trampling, so look for quieter parts of shingle beaches.

Don't confuse with: Field poppies, which have flowers of the same shape but they are red and grow in fields or evening primrose and mulleins, which both have yellow flowers but they grow from a flower spike, not from a rosette.

Wildflowers of grassland

Grasses grow from the base, so that animals nibbling from the top don't harm them. These flowers live among the grass.

Grasses

Grasses aren't just the plants between the wildflowers – they are wildflowers!

Meadow foxtail (up to 1m tall)

Identification: The flower heads do look like the tails of very tiny foxes.

Fact: Flowers early in the year and often causes the first flush of hay fever for sufferers.

Uses: Grown for animals to eat and to store as hay for winter food.

Where to see it: In farmland and along road verges throughout the UK.

Don't confuse with: There are two similar species of grass among our 200 or so similar grasses, rushes and sedges.

Common reed (up to 3m tall)

Identification: This is the plant that makes up reedbeds, an important habitat for wildlife. It grows in dense patches in wetlands, along riverbanks and can even cope with salt water in estuaries.

Fact: In the right conditions, common reed can spread up to three metres a year, so it can swamp an area if left undisturbed.

Uses: As well as being a great habitat for wildlife, common reeds are used for thatching roofs.

Where to see it: Along slow rivers and the edges of lakes, but at its best in nature reserves.

Don't confuse with: Planted crops of sweetcorn or wheat, because they grow so densely.

White clover (flowers 1.5-2cm across)

Identification: White pompom flowers that may have a pink tinge. Leaves have three lobes, but finding four-leaved versions is considered lucky.

Fact: Clovers have the ability to take nitrogen gas from the air and fix it in their roots whereas most plants have to take nitrogen from the soil. This means that clover can grow in poorer soil than many plants.

Uses: White clover is grown as a green manure, but is also prized by beekeepers because it produces lots of nectar for their bees to make honey from.

Where to see it: Most grasslands, including lawns, will have clover in them, but it may be mown before it flowers. Look for darker patches in the lawn and then spot the leaves.

Don't confuse with: Red clover, which is much taller and has red flowers.

Common spotted orchid (up to 40cm tall)

Identification: One tall flower spike per plant rising straight up from a rosette of oval-spotted leaves. Individual flowers can range from white via the more usual pale pink to purple.

Fact: Orchids produce some of the smallest seeds in the plant world, and depend on a fungus to help them grow – no fungus, no orchid.

Uses: This is one of the few wildflowers that looks so exotic that people grow it for the simple enjoyment of its appearance.

Where to see it: Throughout the UK, mainly on damp grassland and even into open woodland, but especially on chalky soils.

Don't confuse with: Heath spotted orchid, which has round spots on its leaves, or fragrant orchid (it smells lovely!) which has spotless leaves. There are over 50 kinds of orchid in the UK.

Wildflowers of heathland

These flowers have to live in very poor, often quite acidic soils.

Round-leaved sundew (rosette up to 5cm)

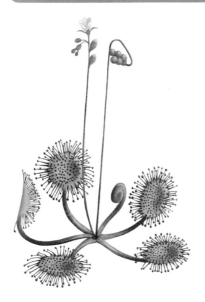

Identification: Round, crimson leaves, each dotted with glistening sticky droplets.

Fact: Sundews need insects to supplement their diets, but don't need them to pollinate their flowers – they can do that themselves.

Uses: This plant is a fly killer! Its sticky leaves trap insects and then digest them to supplement its diet.

Where to see it: On bogs, fens and heathlands throughout the UK. Look around the edges of heathland ponds because sundews like wet feet.

Don't confuse with: The other species of sundews in the UK have different-shaped leaves, but all look quite similar.

Bell heather (up to 60cm tall)

Identification: Thin, needle-like leaves on a low bushy plant, but distinctive small bell or lantern-shaped pink flowers.

Fact: This flower lives on poor heathland soils, but is particularly found on the drier parts of the heath. It's not unusual to see it growing along the side of heathland paths because people choose the drier places to walk too.

Uses: Bell heather plants were used to make animal bedding and brooms.

Where to see it: On dry heaths throughout the UK, but it is also grown in rockeries.

Don't confuse with: Ling, or common heather, which looks similarly bushy, but has tiny, open pink flowers with four petals.

Wildflowers of woodland

These usually flower early in the year, before the tree leaves block out the light.

Primrose (plant 10cm tall)

Identification: Rosette of slightly crinkly pale green leaves, with up to a dozen or so delicate pale yellow flowers growing one per stem from the centre.

Fact: Look closely at the flowers on different plants and you will see they come in two types, called pin and thrum. They have to mate with each other.

Uses: The flowers used to be made into a country wine and some people used to eat the leaves, but primroses aren't as common as they used to be, so leave them for everyone to enjoy.

Where to see it: In woodland and old hedgerows, flowering in early spring before the tree canopy comes into leaf.

Don't confuse with: The cowslip, which is a darker yellow and has several flowers on each stem.

Wood anemone (up to 30cm tall)

Identification: Six petals (but sometimes more) on a white flower. Leaves look rather ragged.

Fact: The flowers open in the sunshine and track the movement of the sun across the sky. In dull or wet weather, they remain closed with their heads down.

Uses: Although the plant is poisonous, it is often grown in parks and gardens as well as living truly wild.

Where to see it: In damp mixed or deciduous woodland or old hedgerows and country road verges throughout the UK.

Don't confuse with: The flowers are much bigger than the other white flowers that grow in similar places, such as greater stitchwort.

Wildflowers of waste ground

These flowers hardly need any soil to grow in – a crack in hard ground is enough.

Rosebay-willowherb or fireweed (up to 2m tall)

Identification: Tall, upright plant with small pink flowers. More often growing in drifts than on its own.

Fact: Colonises bare ground such as fire sites. Spread rapidly in the UK in the 18th century, following the development of the railway network, and again following the bombing of World War II.

Uses: Young leaves used to be eaten by Native Americans but more rarely in the UK.

Where to see it: Any bare or disturbed ground, such as railway tracks, abandoned building sites and new road cuttings.

Don't confuse with: Great and hoary willowherbs, which are both much hairier.

Buddleia (bush up to about 4m high)

Identification: A garden escapee so plenty of varieties. Most common has cone-like clusters of small purple or white flowers.

Fact: Pushes its way into cracks in concrete and pavements, especially in waste ground.

Uses: Widely planted as a garden plant to attract feeding butterflies, which most varieties do well, but it's useless for most caterpillars.

Where to see it: Almost anywhere in towns and cities, even growing out of old walls and chimneys!

Don't confuse with: Other bushy garden escapes such as lilac.

Lower plants

Not lower to the ground, just more primitive. They don't flower but are just as interesting. They include mosses, ferns and seaweeds.

Hart's-tongue fern (leaves up to 60cm long)

Identification: A wavy rosette of bright green leaves all year round, with scribbly brown markings underneath.

Behaviour: Grows in dark damp places, such as on canal lock gates, wet country lanes, river banks and dark woodland.

Uses: It used to be made into a medicine to treat all sorts of ailments, but it may not have worked at all.

Where to see it: Grows throughout the UK, but is less common in the far north.

Don't confuse with: There are over 60 different wild ferns in the UK, but the hart's tongue is distinctive.

Sphagnum bog moss (leaves a few mm long)

Identification: Sphagnum can be red, yellow, brown or green. It grows in great multi-coloured carpets as the main plant of many of our uplands.

Behaviour: Sphagnum is the main bog plant and holds a huge amount of water.

Uses: Sphagnum rots down to form peat, which is used as a fuel or for planting garden flowers. It is much better left in the wild, though.

Where to see it: Bogs and uplands across the UK are covered in sphagnums.

Don't confuse with: There are at least 10 similar sphagnum species in the UK and perhaps 300 worldwide.

Bladder wrack (up to 40cm long)

Identification: A strong central rib and round, marble-sized bladders make this green or black seaweed stand out.

Fact: Clings to stones along sheltered coasts. Its bladders help it to float in the water to get as much light as possible.

Uses: This was the original source of iodine that was used to treat people with thyroid problems.

Where to see it: Mainly on sheltered North Sea coasts, but you can find it on the tideline anywhere.

Don't confuse with: Rockweed, which has slimmer fronds and egg-shaped bladders.

Sea belt (up to 3m long)

Identification: Broad but crinkly-looking brown seaweed, sometimes washed up after a storm.

Fact: Grows from just below low tide to around 30m deep and sometimes attaches itself to big rocks rather than the seabed.

Uses: Was a source of sweetener during World War II.

Where to see it: Washed up on a beach anywhere around our coasts.

Don't confuse with: The other big seaweeds, such as oarweed, which don't have the wavy form.

Fungi

Are they animals? Certainly not. Are they plants? Hmm, much trickier. Many people think fungi are plants because they mostly grow from the ground and don't move around much. But really they are separate, neither animal nor plant, a group of their own.

The fungi we see are usually just like the fruits on an apple tree. The main fungus itself remains hidden within the soil or growing through the rotting wood of a tree. It's there all year, but we mostly see fungi in the autumn, especially after rain, when most of them pop up very quickly as mushrooms or toadstools. Others, such as the bracket fungi or the blobby King Alfred's cakes, can be seen all year round.

Be careful

Some fungi are great to eat, others would make you sick, and taking even a small bite from some would see you die a horrible, painful death. Some of the really nasty ones look and even smell very much like the edible ones. It's safer not to eat any wild fungi at all. And remember to wash your hands after touching any fungi.

Identifying fungi can be really difficult, but a few things to look for are the overall shape and colour, how the underside of the cap of the toadstools looks, and the colour of the spores. Spores are like a fungus's seeds. Take a fresh toadstool cap, put it on white paper and leave it overnight, covered with a bowl. In the morning, some of the spores will have dropped onto the paper in an interesting pattern. You can preserve this with a little bit of hairspray.

Remember to wash your hands after touching any fungi, like this shaggy ink cap.

Mushrooms and toadstools are nature's great recyclers, breaking dead things down for regrowth.

Fly agaric (up to 30cm across)

Identification: The classic fairytale toadstool, usually with white spots on the red cap. White stem with a frill near the top.

Uses: In olden days, it was used to kill insects in milk.

Fact: This toadstool is poisonous but very rarely kills people because it is so easy to identify – unless its white spots have rubbed off in the rain!

Where to see it: In woodlands or old grasslands across the UK. It lives on both pine and broad-leaved tree roots.

Don't confuse with: There are many other red toadstools and other more dangerous species in the same family but they have pale caps.

Giant puffball (up to 70cm across)

Identification: A huge pale ball of a fungus that may be either out in the open in a meadow or hidden in a woodland.

Uses: Fresh giant puffballs can be eaten, but they often get used as footballs!

Fact: If all the spores in a single giant puffball grew up, they would weigh more than the whole world – clearly they don't!

Where to see it: Never common, but in meadows, hedgerows and woodlands throughout the UK from late summer.

Don't confuse with: Very young ones may look like smaller fungi, but fully grown they may look like a football!

Sulphur tuft (up to 6cm across)

Identification: Bright yellow fungus, usually more orange in the centre and paler around the edge. Grows in bunches, often the only fungus around.

Uses: Foresters may be able to use sulphur-tuft to help wipe out a fungal disease of pine trees.

Fact: Like many of our fungi, sulphur tuft is bitter-tasting and poisonous.

Where to see it: Grows from rotting wood, usually near the ground. Common on old logs or rotting tree stumps throughout the UK.

Don't confuse with: There are over 15,000 species of fungi in the UK, but the one most similar to this is conifer tuft, which is browner and lives only in pinewoods.

Birch bracket (up to 30cm across)

Identification: Pale brown on top and white and spongy looking underneath, rather than frilly like the other fungi in this book.

Uses: This fungus was used to sharpen old cut-throat razors. It is sometimes called 'razor-strop'.

Fact: It always grows with the spongy underside facing downwards, so if you find one on the ground on a branch, you can work out which angle it grew at.

Where to see it: On old, sickly and dead birch trees throughout the UK.

Don't confuse with: There are many other bracket fungi, but this is the most common, so long as you are looking at the right sort of tree.

Glossary

Bivalve – a shellfish with two shells, usually of the same shape.

Bracket fungus – a fungus that grow from the side of a rotting tree or old stump, often looking a bit like a shelf.

Broad-leaved tree – one with wider leaves than pine needles. Most drop them for the winter (except holly).

Carnivorous – meat-eating, and often without eating much else.

Clearfell – an area in a woodland where all the trees have just been removed.

Cold-blooded – all creatures except birds and mammals need to use the sun's heat to warm up so they can move around. This is known as being cold-blooded.

Crepuscular – active at dawn and dusk.

Crofting – farming life on some Scottish islands.

Deciduous – of trees, having leaves that all fall off together in the autumn.

Diurnal – active during the day.

Dorsal fin – the fin on the back of a fish, dolphin or whale. You won't see one on a seal.

Dune slack – the marshy area behind some sand dunes.

Field guide – a book that helps you to identify wildlife.

Habitat – the type of place that a creature lives in, such as a woodland or rockpool.

Hide – somewhere to sit and wait for wildlife, where you can see out, but creatures cannot see in very well.

Hover – the flying equivalent of running on the spot.

Hybrid – an animal or plant whose parents are two different species. Most animal hybrids can't breed themselves.

Insect – a six-legged creature with a three-part body plan. Includes butterflies, ants and beetles, but not spiders.

Insectivorous – of a plant, one that catches and eats insects to help it grow.

Invertebrate – a creature without a backbone. Also known as a minibeast.

Key – a way of finding something out by answering simple questions.

Landscape – what somewhere looks like from a distance.

Maggot – the wriggling legless young grubs of flies or beetles.

Glossary

Migration – the regular seasonal movement of animals from one part of the world to another. Many birds and insects migrate hundreds or thousands of kilometres every year.

Minibeast – another word for invertebrate. Any small creatures – insect, spider, slug etc. Does not include any vertebrates, however small.

Native – an animal or plant that has either always lived here or arrived under its own power is said to be native.

Nocturnal – active at night.

Plumage – the feathers of a bird seen as a whole. Summer and winter plumages may look very different for some birds.

Poisonous – has harmful or possibly deadly effects when eaten or touched. Some fungi and berries are poisonous, but very little UK wildlife is dangerous.

Predator – any animal that lives by catching and eating other animals.

Reservoir – an artificial lake that people build to collect water.

Rhizomes – fat, root-like parts of plants such as reeds or irises that grow underground before sprouting up as new plants.

Sett – a badger family's underground home.

Species – a group of similar animals or plants that can breed together to produce young, which can then breed themselves. So house sparrows are a species, as are daisies and human beings.

Tentacle – slim flexible tube or arm used for feeding, feeling or moving around. Usually found on invertebrates.

Toadstool – a fungus that looks like a mushroom, with a cap and stem.

Tracks – footprints or an animal pathway.

Ultraviolet light – light that we can't see, but that some animals can, such as moths or blue tits.

Vegetarian – an animal (or person) that eats only or mainly plants.

Vertebrate – an animal with a backbone: mammals, birds, reptiles, amphibians and fishes, but nothing else.

Warm-blooded – being able to work whatever the outside temperature. Birds and mammals are warm-blooded.

Index

Index

Index

RSPB Wildlife Explorers

If you've enjoyed this book, then you'll love RSPB Wildlife Explorers. It's the biggest wildlife club for children in the world!

You'll get some great stuff when you join. For starters, you'll receive your very own membership pack bursting with goodies, plus six magazines a year, each of them packed with fascinating facts, games, competitions and things to do. You'll discover more about amazing wildlife – from skydiving peregrines to hibernating hedgehogs – and learn what to look out for throughout the year, so that you can put your newfound wildlife watching skills into practice.

And becoming a member also means that you'll be helping the RSPB look after nature here in the UK, and around the world. That's everything from puffins nesting on British cliffs to tigers in the rainforests of Sumatra.

So what are you waiting for? Join today and discover a world of wildlife.

Find out more at
www.rspb.org.uk/join

Otter

Acknowledgments

Author: Mark Boyd
Design: Geoff Ward, Tower Designs
Illustrations: Robin Bouttell, Ian Jackson, Sandra Pond, Peter Scott, Chris Shields.

Mark Boyd would like to thank Derek Niemann and Emma Brookman of the RSPB for their help with this book and the Bloomsbury team for giving him the chance to fill the wettest summer on record with writing it. Above all, though, Mark would like to thank his partner, Chris Tucker, for supporting not only the book, but also his obsessive natural history interests over the years, especially when he should have been doing something useful instead.

All photographs © Shutterstock.com except: p27 © Padmayogini/Shutterstock.com; p45 © hazelisles via Wikimedia Commons; p82 © Tony Garrett. Copyright in the photographs remains with the individuals and organisations credited above.

About the author

Mark Boyd has been fascinated by wildlife since he was a very small boy. He grew up in Dorset, where his love of birds, badgers, butterflies and other wildlife flourished. He trained as a bird ringer in his teens, studied Ecology at Loughborough University and wrote his doctorate on primroses at The Open University. Since 1989, he has worked for the RSPB, first as an editor, then web manager, youth manager and, today, as head of youth and education. Throughout that time, he has remained passionate about wildlife. He is still a keen birdwatcher and ringer, and also a regular moth trapper and wildlife artist.

Red admiral butterfly

Other books you may enjoy:

ISBN: 978-0-7136-8795-8

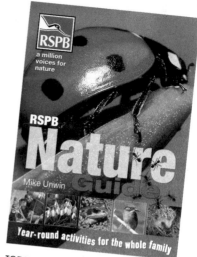

ISBN: 978-1-4081-0514-6

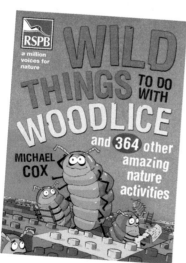

ISBN: 978-1-4081-2783-4

ISBN: 978-1-4081-4821-1